New Hope

How to Live with Power and Purpose

by
Robert Jenkins

Lappidoth Publishing
Rugby, North Dakota

An
Inspiration
by
Lappidoth Publishing

NEW HOPE:
HOW TO LIVE WITH POWER AND PURPOSE

Copyright © 2002 by Robert Jenkins
All rights reserved

Printed in the United States of America
by **Fine Print of Grand Forks, Inc**
4051 Gateway Drive
Grand Forks, ND 58203
701.772.4802

Cover Design: **Go-Go Express** / Margo Sundberg
MSundb9833@aol.com

1st printing 2002

ISBN 0-9720874-2-7

Lappidoth Publishing
PO Box 105
Rugby, North Dakota 58368

lappidoth@stellarnet.com

Contents

Foreword 7

Chapter I.   Hope And Victory 11
You can choose life or you can choose death. The first step is your choice.

Chapter II. Float the Boat 19
In which hope is defined and its various necessary qualities are described. Like a sailing vessel, our hope keeps us afloat as we press into our purpose in life.

Chapter III. The New Millennium 35
In which we learn the first great lesson of hope: I am not in control of anything, except me. Hope floats the ship, but you are the sailor.

Chapter IV. Be a Freedom Freak 49
In which we learn the second great lesson of hope: I am free.

Chapter V. The Unknown:Friend or Foe? 61
In which we learn the third great lesson of hope: Tomorrow is unknown – anything can happen! The bad weather we sail in today will change, so keep on sailing.

Chapter VI. Cultivate Hope 73
In which we understand that hope requires attention. It cannot be taken for granted lest it wither. Hope is worth the time and trouble it takes to make it grow.

Chapter VII. Natural Hope 83
In which hope and wishing are contrasted and we learn that hope is full of promise. Because hope is part of the human condition, it is subject to natural laws. Hope is involved in the "give and take" of energy. Remove the obstacles to hope.

Chapter VIII. Invest the Best 95
In which we apply three principles of investment to maximize the hope that we hold inside.

Chapter IX. Who Are You 103
In which we examine the role of our identity. We are defined by who we are, not by our works. A definite identity is a valuable asset because it relates to our purpose and the promise of hope.

Chapter X. People of Vision 117
In which we learn the value of vision and discover that the vision can be written down and used for our benefit.

Chapter XI. Measure for Success 133
In which we come to see the value of feedback. Knowing our results is absolutely essential to producing good outcomes.

Chapter XII. Dream-Believe-Plan-Do 143
In which we learn the orderly progression of how to turn our dreams into living realities.

Chapter XIII. What Will You? 153
In which we discover the power of the human will. The will is greater than our emotions and intellect – it is the part of us that makes choices.

Chapter XIV. Flames of Desire 167
In which we examine the role that desire plays. Desire, like the mast of a sailing ship, holds the sails open to catch the wind. Our will, like a boom, pivots on the point of our desire.

Chapter XV. Optimism-The Language of Hope 181
In which we examine the role of optimism. What we think and what we say have direct influence on our ability to endure. Hope helps us to endure the testing, because we know we are pursuing our purpose

Chapter XVI. Practical Advice 193
In which we learn that advice – even when unsolicited – is best when it is practical. There are simple things that you can do to improve and maintain the hope in your life.

Chapter XVII. The Three A's for Victory 201
In which we discuss the interaction of a healthy appetite, a positive attitude and a superior altitude with hope.

Chapter XVIII. Hope From The Heart 215
In which we say goodbye with the certain knowledge that hope is worth the effort. Where there's life, there's hope.

Additional Reading 219

Index 220

About the Author 224

Foreword

Once upon a time, a young sailor went off into the far world and wide to make his fortune. He bid the familiar shores of home a fond farewell, hoisted his sails till they were full of breeze, and set a course into uncharted regions of adventure. He knew that he was right. He knew that he was strong. He knew what he wanted and knew he was going to win.

Many years passed before he returned to the shores of all that's known. He was older, and neither he nor his ship had much of the handsome trim they once enjoyed. He was broken, yet far better able to give. Humbled and humiliated, yet far better able to listen and understand. Weakened, yet far better able to care.

He told the folks, down on the docks, a bit of what he'd seen and gained. In all his quest for treasure and glory he had learned that it isn't what you get that counts, it is how you live.

He'd learned that ships are made for sailing, and sailing is meant for getting somewhere. *Where* you choose to go is important. *Why* you choose to go is even more important. Greater still is *how* you choose to sail the craft. The type of vessel you pilot isn't the important thing – sailing is.

Battles and battling had taught him that swords and canons are powerful weapons for good or evil; it is how you use them that make the difference. There is always booty – but the spoils aren't the victory; how you wage your warfare is.

On his way to his mother's house, the sailor chanced upon a child. Bending down he placed a single silver ducat into the young one's hand. "Use it wisely, my little one – but above all, use it. There will be more of these, you'll see." Rounding the bend, the sailor passed beyond the edge of town. Come the next morning, both he and his ship were gone, returned to the seas for sailing.

T he lessons of life are strangely learned. What I know best about life I have apprehended by living. Despite my early convictions, I now know that there are more important things than being right; more important things than being strong; and more important things than getting your own way. Winning isn't a thing to be grasped – it's a way of life.

This book of hope is written in the certain knowledge that no one – least of all me – can guarantee that your adventures will bring you health or wealth or glory. What I *can* guarantee is that **how you live your life will make all the difference**. Hope is a precious gift and what I possess I freely impart to you.

I am grateful to so many for their contributions to me and to this effort. Special thanks are due to my mother, my father (thank you for the edits, encouragement, and ability to make it come alive), my brother Christopher and sister Lynn (who directly helped me when I had no wherewithal), Anna Marie Ettel, Margo Sundberg, Daryl and Cindy Jelsing, my children, and of course, my God.

I dedicate this book to my wife, Debra. There are many women in this world and none her equal. Her capacities to love and care, as well as her sublime patience, have taught me more than all my years of schooling combined. From her encouragement to her thoughtful recommendations, I am happily indebted to her. Together we have faced fair weather and foul, and we have survived the deadly hurricane; through it all she has been faithful, smart, and tenacious. She knows how to "live a little, and hope a lot."

Robert Noel Jenkins

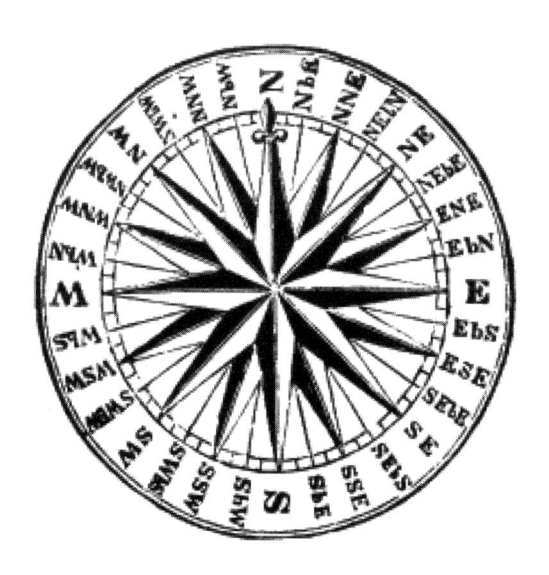

Chapter I

Hope and Victory

The young lady sat across the desk from me, tears in her eyes. Clenching her hands and staring down at the floor, she told me about last night – about how hard she had worked to put a loaded revolver in her mouth and pull the trigger.

I wondered in horror, "Why tell me? Who am I?" I was just her employer, (nowhere near as good a boss as I should have been) and I had never been trained for personal counseling. Her story made me shiver.

She was sad, but strangely calm as she related how hopeless her life was. She knew she was a failure as a person, a nurse, a wife, and a friend. Emotionally she was a wreck, and physically she was completely worn out. What else could she do but rent a motel room, buy a gun, and try to finish it quickly.

"Oh Lisa," (not her real name) "Oh my goodness. I'm so glad you couldn't do it."

"But I tried. I really did. It just wouldn't shoot." Then she laughed bitterly. "Till I threw it on the floor, and it

blew a hole in the wall. I couldn't even kill myself right. But when I saw that hole in the wall, I knew I couldn't do it. I got scared and left that motel as fast as I could. I even threw the gun away.

"What am I going to do now? What can I do?"

How would *you* answer her? You know what came to my mind? The little words my mother always said whenever something went wrong. "Where there's life, there's hope."

"Lisa," I said as I came around the desk. "You can choose life or you can choose death. The first step is your **choice**. And Lisa, **life is *always* the right choice.**"

We agreed on time off from work and she promised that she would see a counselor immediately. (Like anyone who is depressed and thinking about suicide – professional help must be sought on the double.) She was still sad, but determined to do something new with her life.

As a consultant I work with individuals and organizations to increase their effectiveness. There are plenty of people who are efficiency experts, and even more who are accounting wizards, but I'm a person who likes to make things work better. What really turns me on is connecting people to their purpose and seeing their vision come alive. For businesses, as well as individuals, there are few things as exciting as restored passion, mission, and excellence. When we do the right things in the right way for the right reasons, we prosper. That's the beauty of effectiveness.

What's Missing?

It's no secret that certain qualities are essential to success, like the value of excellence (quality workmanship – first and foremost), the value of service (fulfilling other's needs and desires), and the value of commitment (giving your best to the mission, the organization, and your co-workers). Yet, amidst it all there is a disturbing trend.

From management to sales to service - from the halls of government to the floor of the shop - people are trying their best to apply the lessons they've learned about quality and customer service, but at heart they do not expect those lessons to work. People are missing the most important element of all – hope! This is particularly true in American government service.

No one expects the government to really care or to work with efficiency and effectiveness, and few government employees expect to make a significant contribution – not because they are bad people. Rather, they work in a laborious bureaucracy that rarely allows them the satisfying belief that they are making a positive difference.

How did it get to be this way?

Life is tough and getting tougher. We are assaulted every day on every front. Age-old problems of trying to get along have teamed up with sophisticated technology, and we are left behind in the dust.

Money is always a problem. Social structures like marriage, family homes, and community, are neither trusted nor trust-worthy. Schools look like armed camps. Terrorists busily unleash campaigns of fear and mockery because it is easier to destroy than to build. These assaults over the last three decades have eroded our hope.

According to psychologist Martin Seligman Ph.D., we are facing an epidemic of depression.

Depression: A Fact of Modern Life

Depression is a terrible enemy. It attacks twice as many women as men and depression among children (once thought to be an almost impossible circumstance) has escalated at an alarming rate. Every one of us, and everyone that we love, is under attack!

To get a sense of how widespread depression has become, imagine standing in the courtyard of a shopping mall and 100 total strangers surround you. Even though you don't know them personally, you can know them statistically:

➢ 25 of them are currently experiencing mild depression (the kind of depression that occurs when you lose a job, have a health problem, fight with someone you love, or experience some kind of loss).

➢ The women you see who were born after 1950 are ten times more likely to suffer depression than women of the generations before them.

➢ 9 of the adults around you will experience clinical depression during the course of any given year.

➢ About a fourth are generally optimistic, a half are average (neither a full-blown optimist nor pessimist), and a fourth are basically pessimistic in their outlook.

➢ The pessimists are much more likely to suffer clinical depression – to have mild depression plummet to **severe depression**, and to be **depressed more often** than the others are.

Our society has spent an incredible amount of time, money, and educational effort to get people to feel good about themselves, without addressing the fundamental basics of our nature, that "feeling swell" and having hope are actually two very different things.

It is entirely possible to feel bad, and yet be buoyed up with great hope, and just as possible to feel good, yet lack the hope we need to get over the next hurdle. Living our modern lives is very tough, and survival is simply not an adequate goal.

Like a slide down a slippery hill, we seem destined to race toward rock bottom. We are often haunted by the thought that we have missed something important, something essential to having a good life. We work harder (sometimes even smarter and faster), yet do we enjoy our labor? What's worse, is when people are truly hopeless, they simply lack the strength and motivation to attempt to reach for all that they could be. It is a sad fact: nothing destroys our potential more completely than loss of hope.

We are often haunted by the thought that we have missed something important, something essential to having a good life.

That's not how it has to be!

You Can Be Full of Hope

It's never too late to get hope, no matter how hopeless you may be. Hope is always worth the effort. When we walk as people of hope we have a sense of promise and purpose that propels us through the dry, hard times. Even when we reach those points where our emotions are played out and our brains are burned out, hope helps us go forward with a will, because we know (with knowledge deeper than mere fact) that tomorrow will come and **anything** can happen.

Do you feel you are a "dollar short and a day late" when it comes to hope? Are the people around you aimless and hopeless, always talking about what they lack, rather than what they have to offer? Have things have been so bad for so long you don't have an ounce of hope left in you? Take heart – hope isn't gone for good.

The first step to a life full of hope is found in recognizing and embracing TRUTH. So here it is – practical truth, front and center.

Lost Hope Can Be Found

Troubles may be mandatory, hopelessness is optional.

If you had hope and can't seem to find where you mislaid it, do not despair. Hope is resilient and will come back to you if you seek it. Hope is just as much a part of the human condition as suffering is. You can find your lost hope.

Hope is available if you take action to go and get it. Damaged hope can be restored. The vessel of hope can be filled to overflowing; you can have more than enough hope to share with others. Better yet, whenever you need hope, you can get it.

Chapter 1: Hope and Victory

Your hope may have suffered injury, but it can be healed. It is not gone forever.

Restoring hope is like a good soil reclamation program. It takes some effort to get practical results: stop the erosion, rework the ground, and amend the soil with nutrients.

Sounds like work? Of course, but all such effort is worthwhile, because only reclaimed land will again bear fruit.

Filling your soul with hope isn't a matter of getting better rules to live by; it is getting a better life. Vowing not to "screw up" anymore isn't very helpful, nor is memorizing the "Reach for Success Top Ten List." Success is reached by living well. That's why our goal in all of this will be to "live a little, and hope a lot."

> *... Filling your soul with hope isn't a matter of getting better rules to live by; it is getting a better life.*

By providing simple and direct timeless truths, we'll work to restore the quality of hope to our lives. The world may be busier and more stressful than ever before, but we will find relevance and reward in the truth.

So lean forward, tune in, read on and refresh your soul. A life full of hope is a life worth living.

Because life isn't about self-improvement - **it's about living well.**

HAPPY NEWS: *Some six years after that day with Lisa, I received a phone call from her. Times hadn't always been rosy, yet she told me she found the help she needed, that things were better. Her marriage survived and they have children. Even though everything isn't perfect, her life is good. She thanked me for listening to her that day and for caring. I thanked her for calling to let me know, and I told her how proud I was of her and her good choices – so grateful she chose life.*

Where There's Life, There's Hope!

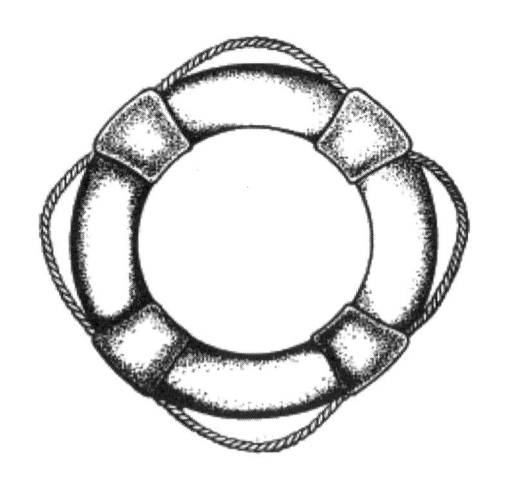

Chapter II

Float the Boat

In which hope is defined and its various necessary qualities are described. Like a sailing vessel, our hope keeps us afloat as we press into our purpose in life.

The central question we'll seek to answer is "How can individuals and their organizations use hope to increase their effectiveness and receive hope to encourage and refresh their soul?" (Yes, I do believe that organizations have a 'soul', although one is never too sure about the Democrat and Republican parties.)

First off, why on earth do we need refreshing?

Because life is tough and we need **to prosper**. We need to do more than just survive, which means we've got to be tougher than the life we've got. If you're trying to hang on with just a survival mentality, I can guarantee that you are already sinking. Survival is not an adequate goal.

The poet Robert Browning said, "a man's reach must exceed his grasp," and he was right. It pays to reach for more than you think you can lay hold of. When you decide to "thrive" you gain a life that will need hope and when you need hope, you can get it.

Hope Defined
So what is hope?

> ➢ It is the sense that something good will come.

> ➢ It is the anticipation that the positive outcome you long for will happen.

> ➢ It is the certainty that good will come even out of the worst circumstances.

> ➢ It is the knowledge that tomorrow is another day and your victory can happen.

Hope is human, and dwells in the very deepest part of us. Hope is personal as well as corporate. Since it is human, it belongs to all human components (singular and plural).

Hope affects our physical self, our thinking self, and our emotional self. Hope is deep and supportive to all we are, all we do, and all we desire. Quality living is full of hope.

There was a movie with the title *Hope Floats* and that title is an accurate analogy of what hope is like. I think hope is best compared to buoyancy – one's ability to float. For a ship, water displacement is everything. Even the heaviest battleship (made out of steel for heaven's sake) floats like a cork because it displaces water with air. Let the air out, and she'll sink like a stone. Your life is like a sailing ship. Hope is your buoyancy. Similarly, you don't create air; you just make sure that you are full of it. You have to make room for buoyancy to have it.

It's worth it. Life on the top of the water is a whole lot more fun and fulfilling than life on the bottom.

The troubles and trials, indeed, all the situations of life (from the surprising to the mundane) are the breeze and the seas. Like good ships piloted by wise Captains, we don't just bob along, suffering the whims of wind and wave to get us some place.

> *Your life is like a sailing ship. Hope is your buoyancy.*

We have a destination in mind, and want to use the elements of the sea to move there.

The Five Necessary Qualities of Hope

Have you ever been sailing? I was born and raised in Minnesota, the land of 10,000 lakes. With all that water around it was impossible not to learn some water sports: swimming, canoeing, even sailing. However, until I actually sailed, I didn't know how it worked.

I had this "kids-eye-view" that it was like turning on a motor and driving straight to wherever you wanted to go.

Wrong! Sailing is completely different because you USE the wind and the waves in order to get to where you want.

There are only five required parts that make up a sailboat:

- some kind of vessel that floats (and this can be as simple as a glorified surf board),
- a sail to catch the wind,
- a mast and boom to maneuver the sail,
- a keel that runs through the middle of the boat into the water,
- and a rudder to steer the ship.

You can use a lot of creativity as to how you design these elements, but you've got to have all five in order to sail. If you are missing even one of them, you won't be able to do it.

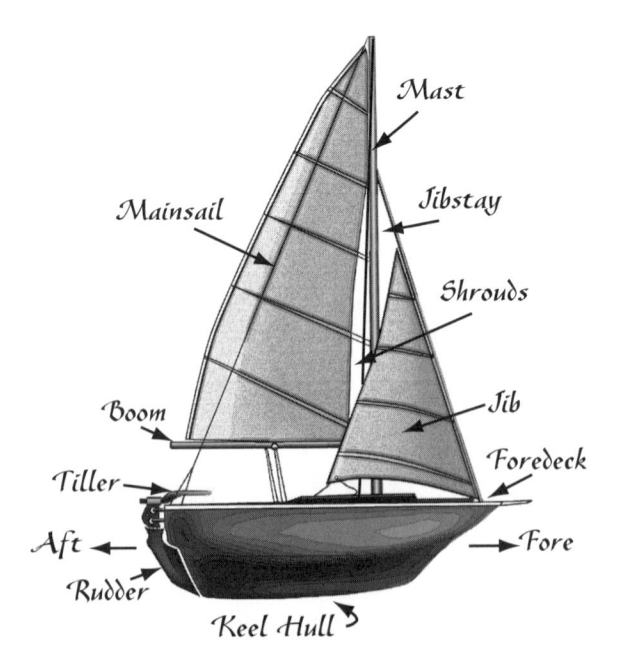

What do each of these elements, these required parts, do for the sailing ship? Let's take them in order.

Floatation

The first one is obvious: without a vessel you have nothing to displace the water and keep you high and dry on top. You have to have a boat to have a boat. (Don't you just love obvious answers?)

Power

Secondly, since we are designing a sailboat, we obviously need the sails. The sails are our "motor" in that they take the energy of our environment and turn it into momentum – movement.

Although I am not a physics professor, I am told that ships do not sail because the wind pushes them, (unless that wind is directly behind them), instead, the wind blows across the sail creating a vacuum on the other side. The boat is actually pulled across the water. The larger the sail, the more vacuum you can create. On really large ships, they use multiple sails to capture a lot of power, like those pictures you've seen of pirate ships.

Flexibility Accesses the Power

Next we need our boom and mast. At the bottom of the sail is the boom, a long rod of metal or wood that is attached to the bottom seam of the sail. The vertical edge of the sail is tied to the mast (as is one end of the boom). Therefore, the mast holds the sail upright in the air, and also acts as the pivot point for the boom. The boom and mast very simply hold the sail open to the wind.

Their second job is to allow the sail to respond directionally to the breeze. Attached to the farthest end of the boom is a line (a rope to you land-lubbers), and by pulling that line you can position the sail tighter against the wind (thereby increasing speed) or relax it (which is very important if you intend to change directions). As the boat changes directions, the boom is able to swing around so that the sail is never useless.

Stability and Commitment
The keel is what you think of as the bottom-most edge of the boat. The keel on a big sailing sloop runs the entire length of the vessel, from the front to the back. On a little sailboat, the keel can be as simple as a center board that drops down through the middle line of the boat into the water. The keel acts like a knife as the boat sails. It gives the boat some "bite" in the water. This allows the boat to keep a forward motion, instead of skittering sideways under a gusty wind.

Direction
Finally, you need a rudder. It is the rudder that steers the ship. Even though the rudder is the littlest part of the boat it performs a vital task. The boat will always go where you direct it; a big push to the left or right will get you a big turn, whereas a little nudge will produce a little turn. As long as the boat is in motion, it will obey the rudder.

Sailboats Enjoy Versatility
Did you know that you can sail into the wind?

Let's say you wanted to cross the lake to the North side, but the wind is blowing directly out of the North. In the ancient days you would have had to wait till the wind changed direction, but with the boom and mast combination, you can harness the power of the wind even when it is against you. Since the wind is coming from the North you "tack" into the wind, which means you sail forward at 45-degree angles to your destination, (see illustration).

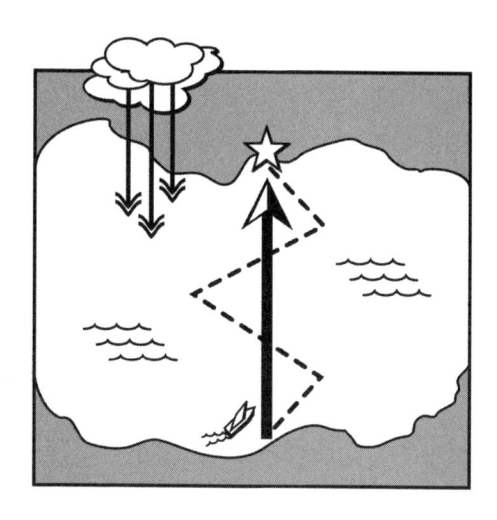

When the wind is from the North, you start by sailing Northeast. This puts the sail at an angle to the wind, which means you are creating a pressure difference (a vacuum) which powers your boat forward.

Of course, if you keep traveling Northeast you'll miss your destination. Therefore, after a time you change the direction of your rudder, aiming the boat at a Northwest angle, and you tack that direction for a while. Thus in small increments you make your way North until you get to where you're going, even though the wind is directly against you.

The Joy of Jibing

The most exhilarating part of sailing is "jibing." When you turn with the wind, the boom sweeps across the vessel, instantly filling the sail as you "run." The sailboat races under the full force of the blow. With the sail set at a 90-degree angle to the wind, your vessel cuts ahead straining to fly.

Speed and Motion

Contrary to common understanding, the boat moves it's fastest when it rides the thin line between a normal tack into the wind and sailing across the wind at a right angle. At that edge of speed, the boat rears up in the water, galloping like a racehorse through the tops of the waves.

If you give too much sail she'll blow you right over into the drink – too little and you'll waste all that speed and power. The thrill is to find the mastery where you are poised on the very edge of risk maximizing every breath.

A Sailor's Two Great Problems

Have you ever been "in the doldrums?" These are portions of the oceans where the breeze hardly ever blows. Sailors dreaded sailing around the world because the doldrums were unavoidable. For days your ship is becalmed, unable to gain any speed or independent direction because there is no wind to work with. You can only sit tight, avoid sunburn, and wait till the ocean's currents slowly take you out.

Sailing can be dangerous no matter where you are on the globe. Sometimes the weather becomes so brutal that the very life of the ship is threatened. No amount of clever sailing can capture the force of those winds or convert the torment of the raging waves. You can only batten down the hatches, reef your sails (tie them up so that they aren't open to the wind), and ride out the storm.

In a storm you try as much as possible to keep your head into the pounding waves, meanwhile bailing water with all your strength. Otherwise, there is no great strategy for sailing through the squalls (other than to avoid them if you are able). Your rudder, sails, mast, boom, and keel are useless. Your only goal is to stay afloat.

The Open Secret of Life
Life is a lot like sailing. There are very few things that are required, but you need to use them all in order to make the most out of your portion.

Hope
The first requirement, like having a vessel, is to have a life. You have to choose life in order to have a life, otherwise, you will eventually have nothing on which to stand – no way to stay high and dry as the trials and circumstances come up. Pick the kind of life you'd like to have and make it buoyant with hope. Your life doesn't have to look like a luxury schooner to justify having hope; it can be a scrappy little "snark", the important thing is to have one and make it float.

One of the great secrets of hope is that it does not rely on our emotions or our brains. Hope is a choice. It relates to our will, (more on this later). Therefore, one has to choose hope to get hope. It will not descend on you from above; it has to be selected. Since you've chosen life, it only makes sense to live hopefully.

Will and Desire
Use your life to your advantage. A quality life uses "living" the same way a quality sailboat uses "sailing." Like the sails to the boat, you need a way to capture the power of your environment in order to go someplace. The winds and waves of our lives are the circumstances in which we find ourselves every hour of every day.

In the same manner that sailing ships use breezes to make progress, you can use the situations and circumstances of living to power your forward motion. Of course this requires that you actually have someplace you'd like to go – a direction. When you know that, you are ready to use the winds of challenge to propel you toward it.

Your will is the sail that catches the energy around you. Your will, raised high on the mast of your desires, is open to take advantage of whatever may come your way because it translates that raw power into something you can use. (Trust me; we'll talk more about this.)

Choice Making

If the mast of your life is your desire and the sail your will, then what is the boom? It is the decisive actions that you take when you make choices. Making choices and pulling them into reality (actually doing something about your choices) is the way you utilize your desire and your will.

Without a course of action, the winds of living simply push the boom in line so that the sail becomes useless. No matter how tall your desire or how nobly large your will, if no one is pulling on the boom to position it to respond to the breeze, you won't go anywhere; you'll waste the energy of your environment. Simply put, our choices convert the environment to our advantage.

Identity

Our identity - who we are in this world and how we see ourselves – is like the keel in that it bites into our environment and keeps us from being blown sideways; it allows the power of the circumstances to move us forward. People who lack an identity, or who have multiple identities, are people who can't hold a straight line in their purpose. They have no "keel" and are thereby blown every which way by living.

Change Making

Lastly (and just as important as the other features) quality life requires that we have something like a rudder. The rudder is our ability to change, to modify our current direction to best use the situations and circumstances of living to get to our destination. The rudder is our connection to our vision, to our dream of what we want to accomplish.

Like a good sailor, we keep a hand on the tiller knowing that as things about us change, we'll need to alter our direction in order to maximize our speed and bearing. Like the boom of **choice** making, **change** making also requires decided action. It can't be left to the brain merely to think about doing something. To use the rudder or the boom, we actually have to DO what we are thinking.

Therefore:

  YOUR HOPE
  + YOUR WILL AND DESIRES
  + YOUR CHOICES
  + YOUR IDENTITY
  + YOUR DIRECTION
  ─────────────────

  YOUR LIFE

Handling the Tough Stuff

Like sailing ships, most of the weather we face is relatively calm and expected. We don't have to think much about what we are doing. The majority of our sailing is into the wind. Thus we make decisions and changes using little course corrections in order to get the most out of our environment.

To the untrained eye, it looks like we don't know where we're going. What we're really doing is "tacking" into the wind, always moving in a general bearing toward our destination.

There are those wonderful times when everything is going our way. All the circumstances are favorable, people are interested and supportive in what we are doing, and we are on an emotional high. That's when we are "jibing" through life.

Like a sailboat at top speed crossing a strong wind, life is risky even when it is fortunate. But oh my, what a wonderful problem to have. Life is rarely so exhilarating as when everything is blowing our way. However, if we let it go to our heads, it's like tipping over in the water. We get soaking wet and have to right our vessel and start all over again. On the other hand, if we get fearful, we slacken the sails and let most of the favorable winds pass us by; we lose all the extra speed and distance. Life is full of risks, and good sailors use the risks they encounter, every day.

> *The doldrums are a severe testing.... if we pass, we find that we are better for the experience.*

Nevertheless, there are those periods or seasons when we face a sailor's two greatest enemies: the doldrums and the hurricane.

The Doldrums of Life

Just like the tropical doldrums, we hit patches without any energy in them. Everything is boring and listless, nothing seems to matter. Emotionally we are at a standstill, and no amount of lecturing seems to get our gumption up at all. What's going on?

Frankly, life can become full of drudgery. There are some people who think the total absence of conflict and challenge equals total peace. I beg to differ with them. Without some kind of energy in our environment, we lack the ability to produce motion in any direction.

The doldrums are a severe testing. Like every other test in our lives, if we pass, we find that we are better for the experience. The important thing to remember about the doldrums is that even though it seems like nothing is changing or growing or improving, slowly and surely we are moving on an unseen current. If we endure we will make it out the other side and be nearer our target. If we turn around or quit, we will have really failed. These dry times are very difficult because they test our resolve more completely than any other situation.

Fear and Faith

Doldrums are frustrating, but violent storms are terrifying.

Nothing is as scary or dangerous as the hurricanes of life. Quicker than a heartbeat, we discover ourselves overwhelmed by life-threatening storms, full of perilous circumstances and situations. These are the times when our best friends desert us, our families disown us, and our sanity is held together by a single thread. No one is supportive or kind.

Our emotions are raw and on edge, our physical bodies are tense and anxious. We hardly sleep, while our brains work overtime without coming up with one useful idea. Everything is out of control and there's nothing we can do to stop it. In its worst state, it is actually deadly, (accidents, disease, and war). At its best, it is cruel and merciless.

This type of testing is holistic: it comes against every part of our person. The storms don't care how noble or important your quest is; *you* don't matter at all. So if *you* don't care about surviving and thriving, nobody will.

This test is more than difficult. Beyond the outside dangers, there is the threat from the inside. In the midst of the storm, we keep hearing that small voice in the back of our brains accusing us, "If you hadn't come out here in the first place we'd be OK. Retreat. Run. No destination is worth it."

Doldrums and hurricanes have essentially the same solution. Do what you can do to hold your "ship" together, and wait it out. The weather is against you for a moment; however, like any natural phenomenon, there is an end to it. It will not last forever. Freakish weather may be uncomfortable, risky, and out of control, but it must be endured. Wait patiently and you will see the circumstances change. Do what you have to do to preserve the integrity of your life and relax as best you can. When the uncontrollable problems pass, you will be able to make repairs and resume your journey.

Life is not about self-improvement - **it's about living well.**

Chapter 2: Float the Boat

Hope is a quality that keeps our life afloat. Hope feels good, treats our bodies well, and is pleasing to think about – yet hope is deeper and more substantial than our feelings and thoughts. Hope sustains us as whole people, and like a boat on the seas, there is no substitute for flotation.

Chapter III

The New Millennium

> In which we learn
> the first great lesson of hope:
> I am not in control of anything,
> except me.
> Hope floats the ship,
> but you are the sailor.

The new century may look scary (and in many ways it *is* scary), but I have great hope for all that is coming, even though I don't know what it is. Hope gets "in the face" of the unknown. Hope is very powerful. It sustains you when there aren't any tangible things to hang on to.

Many times we plant our feet and just refuse to budge until we "understand" why we have to change, or until we "understand" what exactly that change will be.

The truth is when we face the unknown, there is no way that we can understand it – it's unknown! If we plant our feet, we'll lose the ability to move with the changes. Even when a change is a bad one, (and believe me, not all change is good), waiting to go until we "understand" is losing precious time. We fall behind.

Take a moment and think about your own life. Recall those times when you had to make some small change. Go ahead, pick a couple that were negative, (meaning that you hadn't planned them, wanted them, or appreciated them). Looking back on those changes, how did you survive? What did you do to finally get over them, or to turn them into something positive and productive? Did you discover that by pushing through those changes, even when your feelings were hurt, you somehow grew as a person?

Life is sometimes like early morning exercising. You start with stretching; otherwise you'll hurt yourself when you get in the thick of the workout. When we stretch we reach beyond our limits. We don't have to stretch so far that it hurts, but far enough that we are leaning against the natural tension and resistance.

Because we do physical stretching we are more limber. We gain a greater range of motion, and we protect ourselves by loosening our tight muscles and tendons.

What would happen if we thought about the rest of our life in the same way? Perhaps we'd be less angry at the little changes if we recognized that they are getting us ready to do some real living – they are helping us limber up so that we aren't crippled by the big things.

Let's Get Personal

Remember the Y2K Bug? That was an interesting time. The "Naysayers" were out there "naying", and the bright, wide-eyed optimists were simply ignoring the whole thing, "If we just talk kindly to our plants and our computers they will be OK."

In the medical profession we had to take that deal very seriously. I mean, you wouldn't want to have to make a call, "Mrs. Smedley? Your husband was doing great, recovering like a champion, and then this small glitch, well, a mere software error, and the respirator sucked out his lungs and mailed them to Chicago."

So we were working very hard to make sure nothing would go wrong. When you have to take control you just go and take control! Right? We were spending a fortune in new software, new processors, new chips, and new systems. The hospital industry in itself must have generated untold billions of dollars of business for manufacturers. (You see, every dark cloud has a silver lining!)

Then came the fateful day. Plant Operations people sat up all night, waiting for the unforeseen to suddenly appear ... and nothing happened. Heart lung machines kept pumping, monitors kept monitoring, and even the Social Security Administration managed to mail out the checks on time. Either we were very successful, or the whole deal was a lot of hooey.

In any case, I worked hard to make sure that Y2K wasn't going to ruin my life. Professionally or personally. Yes sir, I even checked out my computers at home to be sure they'd operate. I was *so* compliant, the very picture of active planning – I ought to have been the centerfold for *Contolboy* magazine.

However, there were a few things I never thought to make Y2K compliant.

What you are about to read is true. No names have been changed to protect the innocent, because we were guilty. Moreover, I swear, nothing is embellished – OK, it may be embellished, but it really happened, and all on the same day!

When I woke up on January 1st, of the year 2000, the first thing I did was to put on my glasses and they broke in half, right at the bridge.

My glasses were not Y2K compliant.

As I was preparing breakfast for the children, I reached up into the cupboard and pulled out one of those bagged cereals and *Cocoa Bombs* came pouring out from one end of the bottom corner of the bag. "That's odd," thought I, as I reached for another bag, "That must have gotten damaged somehow." Pulling out a new bag of *Frosty Coated Sugar Sweeties* it also had a hole in the same lower corner, as if something had chewed it open. Great hunter that I am, I climbed a chair and peered into the depths of the high cupboard. Sure enough, physical evidence confirmed the awful reality – we had a mouse in the cupboard!

Even my cabinetry wasn't Y2K compliant.

Then a voice rose from the basement. "Dad, there's a BM floating in the shower!"

This did not sound good.

Further detective work revealed that the entire city of Rugby, North Dakota was backing up into my sewer with a vengeance.

My plumbing was definitely NOT Y2K compliant.

Quick phone calls soon had me in possession of about 3,000 pounds of roto-rooter equipment. As I lugged it downstairs, my wife was coaching me from the top landing, saying something helpful like, "Are you sure you know what you're doing?" When suddenly, her back molar broke in half and she swallowed it.

Never in my wildest imagination did I consider making her teeth Y2K compliant!

Despite these disasters and the cold outside, I knew we'd stay warm - by the flickering glow of the microwave oven as it burst into flames that afternoon.

Two days later on January 3rd I went to work and learned that my job was eliminated. I was "downsized!"

Why is it that when you're downsized your waistline gets up-sized, and your finances are capsized because you have to buy new clothes that are rightsized?

In spite of all my careful planning, in spite of my remarkable brainpower, in spite of taking logical precautions, and in spite of my driving need to control every circumstance, even my job was not Y2K compliant!

How could I have foreseen these changes and what could I have done about them? Frankly, nothing. That's the way life goes. As my Dad would say, you have to play the cards you are dealt. (And this wasn't a time for bluffing.)

Looking back over the history of the world, (and since I hadn't a job I had plenty of time for historical reflection), I saw in a flash that nothing is certain. Everything is subject to change.

The Change Factor

Have you noticed that most changes come all on their own? Very few are planned or mapped out. Most major changes that I have faced in my job or in my relationships come from outside of me. More often than not, I only get to react to change.

This is not to say that I'm not trying to be proactive. I am a goal setter by nature, and enjoy designing new challenges (from the easy to the wild and wacky), and yet, no matter how I make my predictions, life has a will all its own. It is chock full o' change.

Change is an animal. Not a nice domesticated breed like a milk cow, but a big untamed, twisting serpent.

Change is an animal. Not a nice domesticated breed like a milk cow, but a big untamed, twisting serpent. Just when you think you've got it by the head, it wraps its tail around you and starts squeezing the daylights out of you. You can fight it or plead with it, but all it says is "Hisssss…" as it does something radically different than you expect.

It's a small comfort, but I am not the first person to make the discovery that change happens. I am **not** in control of circumstances or of other people. Decisions are made constantly, some by me and some by others, and for every decision that is executed, certain paths are opened while others are blocked off, forever lost.

Chapter 3: The New Millennium

Sometimes I appreciate that, but most often I resent the heck out of change.

It's an interesting fact that the folks of the Meninger Clinic could all agree on one point, that all change is perceived as loss.

All change is perceived as loss, and the emotional response is ANGER!

That explains the weird feelings you have when something good comes along and you still find inside that you're feeling kind of "funny." What you're missing is the way things were.

Good or bad, wanted or unwanted, needed or feared, when change happens to a human being, we respond to the **loss of what we once had** rather than to the **opportunity** we are suddenly granted.

Now, I could have sat around bemoaning the fact that I never went off to Los Angeles to become a famous waiter waiting to become a famous actor. I could have been depressed because I hadn't seen it coming or I could have hated myself because I hadn't gotten a different job first and told *them* where to get off. I could have just given up and gone on welfare, spending the rest of my life in pajamas, reading the want ads wondering why no one calls on the phone.

Instead, I made a decision to capitalize on the change that had been dealt to me. Like the old saying goes, "If life gives you lemons, make lemonade."

To have a quality life, I had to make choices. Life may suck, or it may be "fat city" – the choice as to what I'm going to make out of it is my choice – mine alone.

The first great lesson of hope is: I am not in control of anything except me. Since I can't control the external environment or other people, I can only control my insides. I can exercise SELF-CONTROL.

It's the same for you. You are not in control of anything except YOU.

You may labor to exercise control and you may have a job that involves taking control of situations, but in reality we are not "in control." When people talk about controlling the work place, they really mean having someone responsible to make choices, reacting to the changes that occur every day.

> *The first great lesson of hope is: I am not in control of anything except me.*

You may be responsible to keep a certain machine working, but you don't control it. It will not obey your every command. If a machine won't obey your will, what makes you think a person is going to? People have free will, and do things because they WILL to do them. At this point machines don't have a will (I know, don't tell that to the copy machine or it will surely jam and destroy your document). As complicated as tools can be, they aren't near as complicated as you or I.

This truth is clear for us as individuals, as it is for society. We really don't control others. Even if you are an elected official, you are not in control of the country, the legal system, or the economy. You may be highly responsible, but you can only control what **you** do and say. The mark of a great leader isn't the genius to force others to stay within certain boundaries; it is the ability to raise people who will exercise their own self-control in order to achieve the best outcomes.

Oppression and Manipulation

I can hear some of you right now thinking, "What about dictatorships or fascist regimes? They make people do all sorts of things because the will of the state demands it. How do you explain that?"

That kind of control is called "Oppression," and if you look at history you will see that oppression only works as long as you can maintain a huge level of fear, spying, and manipulation of a few chosen rewards. But what happens every time that fear is lifted? Everyone goes their own way. The neatly ordered society becomes disordered. After Hitler's death, no one was a Nazi. When Mussolini's power to command the military was gone, the people killed him and hanged his body in the public square. Surprisingly, no one in Italy was a fascist anymore.

A Sad Modern Example

Tito ruled Yugoslavia for a lifetime. All those ethnic groups seemed to get along just fine, as long as they stayed well within the boundaries the secret police set for them. Though he ruled a communist country, even capitalists in the West were amazed at the reconstructed society, the massive building projects, and their economic standard of living.

However, just as soon as the oppression was lifted, what happened? War and ethnic cleansing. The government collapsed, the country broke into small political pieces, and beautiful cities were laid waste as hatreds as old as the crusades flamed into passion. The will of the people hadn't changed for 50 years; it had only lain beneath the surface, waiting to be expressed. When the oppressive regime ended, so had all the visible peace and prosperity.

What Does That Mean to Me?

If you want that kind of home life or work life you may have it. As long as you are willing to oppress those you love and play one against the other, meting out punishments and rewards in order to manipulate them to do what you want when you want it, you can have control. Just don't ever take a vacation, or get sick, or send a kid to college. Don't let your guard down for a moment, because they will all run off willy-nilly and the control you thought you had will have vanished into chaos.

My only question to those people who feel that running their household means making every decision and forcing every spouse and child to do them, is this: "Do you *really* want that kind of relationship?"

People who have to oppress others in order to be in control are constantly in fear of losing that control – and well they should be. The worst part is they never really know if their wife or daughter or son or friends love them. They know that these folks obey because they are oppressed and controlled to obey. They know that if they ever lift that oppression they stand a good chance that these people will flee from them. Therefore, they squeeze down all the harder.

Is that a fair trade, I wonder?

I certainly don't think so. I want to be loved because someone has chosen to love me. I want them to care about me despite all my failings and weaknesses and insensitivity. I want to be able to give love to them and to freely help them, not because I have to, but because I want to.

If you're like me, then you'll have to agree that no one truly controls anyone else. The only control we get to have is **self-control**. And that's hard enough.

I know I'm not the master of my family. A case in point was the day I did one of those father things, where you gather the troops together and issue orders. My wife was out, and I had plans. It only seemed natural that if I had plans everyone else should have plans too – as long as they're my plans.

So I had all five kids in one spot and did the old routine, "You there, go do this and that. And you, hiding behind the couch, you carry all this stuff down to the basement, and you over there, you carry all this other stuff up from the basement. And you scurry fast and pull all those things out, while you over there put all those other things away. Now hurry up, let's get the show on the road."

And no one moved. They simply exchanged looks.

My daughter, the youngest of the crew, looked up at me and said, "Shouldn't we wait till Mom gets home?"

For a moment I couldn't breathe. "Hey," I croaked, "I'm the Dad. I can do this stuff you know. Mom's not the only one around here who can give orders."

She stood up, walked over to me, and patted my arm.

"It's OK, Dad. You're funnier."

Once again I was reminded that just having a title or being in a position of authority is not a "Carte Blanche" card to allow control. I can't control others, and when I think about it, I really don't want to. Just like you, I have to love, and direct, and lead without controlling.

I'm Not in Control, and it's OK

Lesson Number One of Hope is really as simple as this.

I am NOT in control.
    And it's OK.

As my son said to me the other day when I was helpfully yelling at him to get the garbage out:
    "Chill, Dad."

Have you ever had a stress test? They put you on a treadmill, and wire you up with a bunch of electrodes, and tell you to start walking. Before you know it, you're jogging, and then they incline the treadmill so that you're running up hill. This allows them to monitor the responses of your heart.

I think having children is like having the opportunity for multiple stress testing - if they'd only hook up electrodes. All the doctors would have to do is have a child come in and say "Chill out" – it would be equivalent to 15 miles of mountain hiking.

When asked what she does for a living, my wife described her job as "I'm a lifesaver. We have five children and I haven't killed any of them yet."

However, what's really annoying about kids is that they thrust the truth right into your face. I hate that. I hate being corrected when I'm wrong. It doesn't bother me very much when I'm right, but it sure gripes me when I'm wrong and they're right.

So when my son said, "Chill, Dad," I had my little stress test moment, and I survived. I did manage to calm down and the garbage did get taken out. Even though I thought momentarily about how satisfying it might be to wrap my bare hands around his neck, I got through it all right, because *he was right*.

I needed to chill out, and I did. He needed to take out the garbage, and he did – even without my having to control him.

The truth is, we can all benefit by taking a chill pill.

You are the sailor, the Captain, of your ship in life. All the artful use of sail and boom and rudder come from YOU. Great sailors, like great hope-ers, know that they do not control the ocean or the four winds. They can only control their own will and actions.

Hope embraces this truth by owning up to the fact that we will use self-control and simply lay aside the old notion of controlling others. It's what we really want, and it's a wonderful way to turn the stress of life into something productive, healthy, and good.

Life is not about self-improvement – **it's about living well**.

So admit the truth and pick up self-control. It not only works better, it feels better, and it's an essential element of hope.

Chapter IV

Be a Freedom Freak!

In which we learn the second great lesson of hope: I am free.

If you're not in control of what life dishes out to you, then what are you in control of? When you are full of hope, you are in control of yourself. This is particularly important when it comes to handling stress.

I have a colleague who once told me that stress was no more than a fashionable fad. Simply a good excuse for doing bad work.

On one level I have to agree that people who don't care seem to lay all the burden of their failed lives on stress, as if their failure was something separate from them and their decisions. Those folks are just looking for a good "cop out," and blaming stress fits the bill. If they want to be a victim and have people feel sorry for them because life is so tough, then stress is as good an excuse as anything else is. After all, who can be mad at a victim?

What's unfortunate is that these people are robbing themselves of quality living. Because they are afraid to succeed or fail they miss the central point to living – which is making choices.

However, my friend's judgment is far too harsh, because stress is authentic. It isn't just a modern diagnosis for an old problem, and it isn't pretend. It is a very real, life-threatening enemy, and has to be dealt with vigorously or it will vigorously ruin your life.

> *... stress is out there, in abundance, and quality living means having a handle on it.*

It is not my intention to spend a great deal of time on stress, (there are many wonderful books and speakers who address that topic far more comprehensively than I intend to) but it is clear to me that stress is out there, in abundance, and quality living means having a handle on it.

So what is stress? My simple working definition is that stress is the total response of the body and soul of a person to the stimuli of the world. Somebody told me that stress is our interior reaction to living. That's not a bad definition, but stress is more than just internal emotions, for stress affects every part of us. When we are stressed we react in body as well as mind.

I have heard some say that a little stress is good, because it acts like a motivator, it gets you moving. I have also heard others who say that all stress is bad and the goal of life is to eliminate it. I have to say that I can't imagine a life without some stress. The only stress-free folks that I know are in cemeteries. So the solution isn't to get stress out of life, but to deal with the stress that is in life. In other words, use stress the same way that a sailing ship uses the wind and water. Move through it.

Stress is a thief, a robber, and like a mugger in a dark alley, stress attacks us physically, mentally, and emotionally – taking from us what we need for good living.

The Cost of Stress

Make no mistake, stress not only **feels** bad, it **is** bad. When we are stressed our blood pressure goes up and our ability to fight infection goes down. We can easily become physically ill, and great stress over periods of time greatly increases our chances of dying! Even our ability to think is affected because so much of our unconscious and conscious brain is responding to the stress load. We spend the majority of our mental effort just to keep operating. When we are stressed, even the simplest tasks require a lot more attention and work.

Emotionally we turn into a wreck. When under great stress we have a terrible time giving to others and appreciating what they are giving to us. It's like having an "owie" - even when Mommy kisses it, it still hurts. It takes so little to set us off emotionally when we are stressed. We tend to act out in extremes. We either explode and make everyone around us pay for our emotional turmoil, or we shrink inside and hide until it feels safe.

Any Conflict or Change Causes Stress

Stress is certainly caused by the bad things that happen, but good things cause stress too. How many of you have found yourselves each December downtown shopping, thinking, "It's Christmas again! Who has the time? Who has the money? Who needs the aggravation?" And yet, Christmas is a good thing, right?

I was on the Internet and discovered a little stress test. It assigned point values to the various things that can happen in our lives causing stress. The higher the points, the more that life event causes stress. At the end of the test you could add up your stress scores and see how stressed you really were. The test also made predictions about your health and well being based on your score.

I expected to see various problems like:
- the death of a spouse or child,
- divorce,
- loss of friends,
- and illness.

What amazed me was the number of "good things" that cause stress:
- getting married,
- having a baby,
- buying a new home,
- and starting a new job.

Even the good things in life bring stress. Certainly any change, good or bad, will cause stress to raise its horrid head. (When I added up my test scores for all the stressors in my life, I discovered that I should have died two years previously.)

Hope vs. Stress

But who said that stress has to win? Hopeful people experience all the stressors in life, but they do not give in to them. They do not let stress rob them of the hope, health, and happiness that they have.

What do they do that the rest of us want to do?

They set their sights on winning and employ some basic winning strategies – simple tactics that can be applied to turn your life from mere survival to prosperity. You see, they don't have an easier life than you or I, they just have a handle on their life, and we can gain the same handle.

For instance, we have already seen that having hope does not require us to control our environment or our family. It means that we determine to control the only person we really have permission to control – ourselves. A whole lot of stress just falls right off our shoulders the minute we come to that conclusion.

The second great lesson of hope is very simple, and most people think it simplistic. In reality, it is hugely powerful, a veritable battering ram that can bring down every mental door that is locked against it.

Here it is:

**I am free.
YOU are free.**

I'm not telling you how it **should** be, or how it **could** be, I'm telling you how it **is** right now. ***You and I are free***.

We are free to take every experience and grow. We are free to change. Free to love. Free to want the things that we enjoy. Free to make choices.

I am always surprised when I catch myself thinking something like, "This is the way it always has to be. You're a loser. Once again you've blown it and you always will."

That's a lie! There is no bigger lie in all of human interaction. I am free. I **can** change.

Do you ever catch yourself talking down to yourself like that? The things that we think and say are very powerful, and when we think a lie, we begin to live that lie. You will surely make mistakes, you may even do things wrong on purpose, but the reality is you are always free. No one but you made you do those things and no one but you are going to fix them, because you are in control of you and you are free.

> *The things that we think and say are very powerful, and when we think a lie, we begin to live that lie.*

You have free will. Even if you live in an oppressive society, you are free. Your choices are yours to make and yours alone. No one can make them for you.

You can give this remarkable power away. You can say to your husband or your mother or your boss, "Whatever you say. You just tell me what to do, what to think, how to act, and I'll do it." But you have to give it away – they can't take it from you.

Moreover, you are always free to take it back. It's never too late. You can be 60 years old and figure you're the biggest wuss that's ever walked the face of the great, green earth. Yet starting right now, this very moment, you have the freedom to make your own decision. You are free to use your will. I don't care how old, how ill, how stupid, how smart, how ugly, or how pretty – you are free. And if you don't believe that, (and I mean really believe it down deep inside), then it's high time you pulled down the lie and picked up the truth.

"Gosh, Bob. I had no idea it was that easy."

Well, sorry to burst the bubble, I didn't say it was easy. I just said it was true and that there is no time like the present to do something about it.

Apply Your Freedom for the Good

It takes time and energy to apply your freedom. It's like any other learning curve. At first it takes a whole lot of energy and application. Because it's new, you have to teach every part of your brain and body to acquire the new process. But over time, just like learning anything else, as you work at it, it becomes easier and easier, until you are doing it just naturally.

You are free, my friend.

Free "From" and Free "To"

Freedom means that you are free FROM something, and it also means you are free TO DO something. Our freedom is not an escape from bad situations; it is an escape from bad living. Our freedom allows us to actually make decisions and change the world by changing ourselves. We can apply ourselves and satisfy our deepest desires to be real, whole, quality people. Because you are free, you do not have to take what stress dishes out to you. Instead, you can set a course through the stress and aim at what you want.

Stress is a fearsome competitor. It will take whatever you will give it in order to dominate your life. Stress will have no mercy on you. It will not care about you personally or take it easy on you. That is why it is so important to get a hold of the truth, and why people of hope are people of truth.

What You Believe Makes a Difference

When you believe that you **have** to control situations, you will certainly be a stress victim, because the truth is you have no control over them. You are destined to be a failure. As long as you keep looking to how you're going to make others behave, you are bound to worry and stress over every situation, even the ones where things "work out."

Studies at the University of Michigan show that when you smile you actually increase the blood flow through the carotid arteries.

That's why the truth is so liberating. You are not personally responsible to fix the entire world, and you are not in control. It is enough to control yourself.

When you believe that you are **not** free, that you lack the power to change or to make choices, then you are going to be the fool of stress – and you might well become the "tool" of stress in your relationships.

People of hope count on the fact that they are free, because they seek to influence the world by influencing themselves first. The truth of freedom is a powerful deterrent to stress. The ability to change – to make silk purses out of sow's ears and lemonade out of lemons – is key to thriving even in stressful situations.

Humor and Stress

There was a fascinating study done recently that looked at people who had heart attacks. They found that the majority of them had very low humor levels. It's true. They didn't laugh much (and certainly not at themselves) and they had trouble finding humor in anything.

The researchers decided to test a hypothesis. They took these heart attack victims who tested low on humor and high on heart unhealthiness, and they put them through humor training. They worked with them to understand humor and to laugh out loud.

The result was that their health status (and their heart health in particular) improved significantly.

So what can we learn from this?

Crabby people get heart attacks.

No, really. I think the lesson is that humor in the face of stress is a valuable weapon. Even a smile makes a great difference. Studies at the University of Michigan show that when you smile you actually increase the blood flow through the carotid arteries. You physically feel the positive result. When you laugh you are doing even more!

Laughter is the Antidote to Stress

So why does laughter make such a difference in how we handle stress? I believe it comes from two basic facts. The first is physical. Laughter is the exact opposite of stress. It does for your body all the wonderful things that stress doesn't.

Lots of laughing is a good cardiac workout, and every time you laugh you release endorphins in the brain that make you feel better, more relaxed. And if that weren't enough, studies show that when you laugh you produce more T cells. Those are the biological weapons your body uses to fight infections. Each time you laugh you are improving your immune system!

The second reason is more psychological. Laughing out loud is one great way to emotionally proclaim the truth. Even though you don't control the situation, **the situation doesn't control you!**

If you want to live it up a little, it helps to laugh a lot. When we let a big belly laugh escape, especially in the face of impossible odds, it puts all the stress of the problem in perspective. Laughter is our best way of saying, "I am not defined by my problem. I may not be in control, but I'm free."

So many of us want to be happy, but our upbringing may make it hard for us to be humorous. This is particularly true for folks in the Midwest. I had a friend who knew an old Vaudevillian comedian. This guy hated performing in Minneapolis because no matter how hard he worked, he couldn't get folks to laugh.

One night in particular he made up his mind to throw all his best stuff to the audience – he would get them laughing or die trying. Of course, he only got a few modest chuckles. After the show, he was standing backstage, thinking about throwing himself off a cliff, when an old Swede came up to him. "Ya, you were real funny."

"Well, you could have fooled me." The comic sighed sarcastically.

"Oh ya!" The Swede said emphatically. "You were so funny I *almost* laughed."

You see, in that heritage from Northern Europe we measure humor by its closeness to laughter, not by the laughs. We are brought up to keep things understated. For instance, I was watching a World War II special on TV, and a British paratrooper was sharing his story about how he jumped into battle with his unit. Most of his friends and comrades were killed before they hit the ground, while he landed in a tree breaking a number of bones, and he wasn't able to get himself untangled. For two days he was hanging in that tree, in constant danger of being shot, going without food and water.

When help finally arrived they had to manhandle him out of there. He fainted from the pain. The interviewer said with astonishment, "How did you get through it?" He answered, with a polite smile, "It was a rum go."

That, my friends, is understatement!

If you've been raised where having a sense of humor was frowned upon, it will take some work to let the laughter out. You have to consciously give yourself permission to laugh; often, and out loud.

For a few of you, that will be a new experience, while for most folks it will be a rediscovery. Have you ever looked at the statistics about laughter? American kids laugh over 400 times per day. 400 times!

How often do you think American adults laugh? Brace yourself.

On average we laugh only 15 times per day.

What the heck happened to us anyway? It's time to let that kid out, to express ourselves freely and honestly.

Therefore I have quit being a control-freak and I have become a freedom freak. I am altogether sold out to freedom. And when you see me laughing I'm celebrating my freedom – the freedom to express myself.

Your laughter, especially at yourself, will allow you to exercise a good influence on your world by keeping your circumstances separate from who you are.

Life is not about self-improvement – **it's about living well.**

So admit the truth. You are free from the bondage of stress and free to be YOU. Put stress in its proper place (which is under your feet, not over your head). You are free to do it.

Chapter V

The Unknown: Friend or Foe?

> In which we learn
> the third great lesson of hope:
> Tomorrow is unknown —
> anything can happen!
> The bad weather we sail in today
> will change,
> so keep on sailing.

We do not hope for what we already have. Hope works by looking forward into the future, which influences our present living. No one needs to have hope when they already have what they want. Therefore, hope is risky. In order to have hope, you have to want something you don't have, and there are no guarantees that you will get what you want. (Heck, there are no guarantees that what you want is what you really should get anyway.) Hope floats us today, so that we can continue sailing toward our chosen destination.

Even nice wholesome people have lousy things happen in their life. They get sick, they lose their jobs, they have marriage problems, they fight with people they love, they get crabby, they suffer heartbreaks and headaches, and even when they are trying their best to be "good" they are misunderstood and unappreciated. Boy! It's almost enough to make you quit being a nice person.

Bad people have awful things happen to them, too. The storms of life are not governed by our political correctness; they do not care one bit whether we are nice or naughty, rich or poor, glum or gleeful. Life is tough. That is why we need hope, because there are no guarantees. Good things and bad things happen. What separates victorious people is whether they capitalize on the challenges. Do you want to change? Do you want to make the best life possible out of the life that you have? Then you need hope.

Tomorrow is New

Hope tells us this great truth - that tomorrow is another day. The problems and trials we face today are not final. This truth is larger than our limitations. Tomorrow is unwritten and unknown. Anything can happen. You **can** change for the better.

Look at the difference between the sexes. People talk about that as if it were carved in stone. Admittedly, our traits are pretty durable, but change can be made.

For instance, do you know what men hate passionately? They hate to be told they are insensitive. Do you know why?

Because it's ***true***: we **are** insensitive. Who likes to be criticized for what is blatantly true? Not any man I know.

Men Can Be Sensitive

There are few things that strike instant terror in the heart of a man like these simple words:

"Honey, do you know what day this is?"

A foolish man will try to guess. "Umm, my birthday? Gosh, is it the Fourth of July?"

A man (who will spend the rest of his life sleeping in the garage) will answer, "Can't you see I'm watching reruns of *Three's Company*? Talk to me later."

A wise man (and I share this great advice with you at no extra charge) will say, "Why yes, my dear, I know what day it is. But I'd like to hear **you** say it."

In any event, each man who hears the question is inwardly thinking:

"AHHHHHHHHHHHHHHH!"

Men are like two scholars having a discussion. The one says, "The greatest problems in the world are ignorance and apathy." To which the other responds, "I don't know and I don't care. Hand me the remote over there, will ya'."

We don't mean to be insensitive. We just have a one track mind, and it's jumped the rails.

How many times have I cursed myself inwardly when I have forgotten an anniversary or birthday, neglected to congratulate a co-worker when they returned from maternity leave, or ignored the dishes when

I saw the sink was full? I have beaten myself up many, many times for being so dull-witted and slow.

All that misery didn't help me. Self-punishment is no substitute for a change in heart. What I did was to make a choice. I decided that even though I am a man, I **could** do the sensitivity thing. Once I decided to be more sensitive, I found a growing interest in learning HOW to be more sensitive. After all, men may be from Mars (and I may have dropped in from Pluto), but at least I was in orbit.

We Do What We Believe

Hope promotes change because hope is the fertile ground out of which we cultivate our beliefs. When I hope that I can change and make that declaration, I have begun the process of creating new beliefs, new convictions. We know that this works. Unfortunately, most people seem to understand this only in the negative sense. For instance, if we really believe that we are defective, and that good things will only happen for somebody else, then our lives tend to look exactly like that. We act defectively and good things pass us by. When opportunity knocks on the door, we're in the bathtub.

Hope promotes change because hope is the fertile ground out of which we cultivate our beliefs.

What good could be unleashed in our life if we applied that same force of belief in a positive way? When we actually believe that we make a difference, and that good things will happen because we are doing the right things with timeliness, then it follows that we will act that way. We will perform with a level of confidence and anticipation that is uncommon, and uncommon good will catch up to us. We're not waiting for opportunity to knock on the door; we're out there looking for it!

"Hold your horses, Bob Jenkins! Are you saying we should pretend? Even when we are horrible and our lives are miserable, we should just act like everything is hunky dory?"

No, that would be denial. Admittedly there is a power to denying reality; unfortunately, it is the power of UN-reality. Denial is unhealthy because it doesn't deal with whatever needs dealing. Simply saying, "It isn't so," and then acting like we're wildly happy or carefree, will not solve our problems any better than wallowing in the pits of despair and wringing our hands, muttering, "Ain't it awful?"

Hope is optimistic because it understands that today's reality isn't final. Hope does not deny reality. It simply denies the finality of it.

Pay close attention to this. Hope has nothing to do with denial. What powers hope is this simple truth: **tomorrow is unknown**. This is the third great lesson of hope – tomorrow can be anything. You may not be in control, but you are free, and tomorrow is just around the corner.

Hope and Optimism are Related

Hope is optimistic because it understands that today's reality isn't final. Hope does not deny reality. It simply denies the finality of it. Today may be bad, but that does not have anything to do with tomorrow. When I make my declaration that I will be more sensitive, I am still a dunderhead. I haven't gained the skills and experience I need to be sensitive for real. But because I am willing to change and hope for good results, I have created the environment I need in order to make those good things happen. My insensitivity may be very real indeed, but it isn't final.

Rhett Butler may not have given a damn, but Scarlet O'Hara knew that "Tomorrow is another day."

Hope is the connective tissue of the soul; and an awful lot of hope revolves around what psychologists call the "locus of control." In short, it is your personal perspective about living. "Locus" means center or focus. Therefore, the locus of control is where you believe control is located.

Do you believe that you control the forces that determine what happens to you? If so, then you are a person with an "internal locus of control." It is considered internal because you believe that you influence your environment, and that you believe the consequences of your behavior relate to what you have done.

Then there are folks with an "external locus of control." They believe that what happens to them is controlled by forces outside of their influence. They may feel that fate or kismet or plain dumb luck determines what will happen to them; that their own behavior will have little to do with their success or failure.

There is truth in both perspectives, because there are certainly circumstances that happen to us that have no bearing on our behavior. We may have been good as gold when something bad came up unexpectedly and kicked us in the slats. Alternatively, we've all had experiences when we learned that our hard work brought a measure of success. If we hadn't applied ourselves, we'd have been losers.

This I know: hope seems to favor those with an internal locus of control. These people have a general disposition that opens them to possibilities. They feel less like victims of life and more like participants. Although there is nothing inherently wrong with an external locus of control, one needs to temper it with truth. We really are in control of ourselves. Even when we face events that are wildly out of our control.

> ...*hope seems to favor those with an internal locus of control. These people have a general disposition that opens them to possibilities.*

A Good Example

My father had a serious, sudden heart problem, and was dragged to the doctor's office right in the middle of a Florida hurricane! The physician knew it was life and death, and time was running out. My father needed an experimental surgery that was only done by four surgeons in this country, one of whom was in Gainesville, Florida. He was rushed by helicopter to the hospital and went into the OR immediately. During the surgery they had to stop his heart in order to work on it.

At some point in the process a blood clot was thrown off the aorta up the retinal artery, which is right beside the carotid artery that supplies blood to the left half of the brain. It could just have easily been the carotid which got the clot, causing a massive stroke, but the clot went to the left eye, so that he lost most of his sight.

My Dad, one of the original "internal locus of control" people, summed up his whole out of control experience this way, "One eye for one brain. Not a bad exchange."

Quality Life is measured by what You make of it

You see it's not what you get; it's what you make of it. Tomorrow is unwritten in the book of life. You have the pen in your hand. What will you do with it? How will you contribute to the day?

Many of us measure our tomorrows by how our yesterdays went. We feel that our personal history is set in stone, and every day will be just like the one before it. Doesn't history teach us that this is far from the truth? If yesterday were the best predictor of how tomorrow would go, then nothing new would ever occur. Was December 6, 1941 the best predictor of December 7th at Pearl Harbor? (Maybe if you were a Japanese pilot it was, but not if you were American.) Certainly September 10, 2001 never prepared any of us for September 11th.

The Power of Hope is Proven in History

History is full of great stories about the power of hope. One of my favorites involves Alexander the Great. Alexander was a remarkable fellow, surrounded by remarkable people, who took just a handful of years to conquer almost the entire known world! Not bad for a kid from Macedonia.

Alexander had many talents. He was charismatic, and a good organizer. He managed to rally his troops into a solid victorious corps. He liked to use innovations to increase their effectiveness on the field of battle, and he was a great leader who thought nothing of getting his hands dirty.

Above all, Alexander was a wonderful hope-er. This guy could hope beyond all odds. In part he knew he needed to set a good example for his troops, but largely his hope sprang out of his unerring sense that he was destined to do something

Chapter 5: The Unknown: Friend or Foe?

EXTRAORDINARY. (He isn't called Alexander the Great for nothing.)

The date was September 29, 331 BC. The place was Gaugamela. Alexander had squared off against the largest world power on the face of the globe, the kingdom of Persia, under the rule of King Darius. For weeks, Alexander had been playing a cat and mouse game with his enemies, each trying to trap the other in unfavorable terrain. Today it was clear that Darius had won the first round.

> *Alexander was a remarkable fellow... who took just a handful of years to conquer almost the entire known world! Not bad for a kid from Macedonia.*

All that day Alexander surveyed the Persian forces, which surrounded him on three sides. He was clearly outnumbered, at least 5 to 1. Worse yet, the Persians had 10 times more cavalry than Alexander. That meant they were more mobile, quicker, and deadlier. The more Alexander scrutinized the Persian forces, the more he disliked them. Even the weather was bad, unearthly hot and stifling.

Alexander prepared as best he could. He studied many different strategies, and finally, late at night, the simplest strategy seemed the best. It was going to be risky, and clearly if he was wrong, all would be lost. He would be fortunate indeed to escape with his life. Yet he knew that the battle does not always go to the strong nor the race to the swift. Tomorrow was going to be another day, and ANYTHING COULD HAPPEN!

What would you do? Alexander the Great went to bed.

In fact, he overslept.

His men finally woke him up. "Gosh, Alex. Maybe you hadn't noticed but there's going to be this huge battle and you're the only guy who has a plan." Alexander the Great wasn't daunted. As he looked out over the mighty Persian army, he exclaimed, "By Hercules, Darius did just what I wanted." You can imagine the effect that his bold, confident hope had on the men.

Alexander wasn't fazed because he knew that Darius already outflanked him on the left and on the right. Normally, you never want to be flanked in battle, but Alexander figured that as soon as Darius sent his cavalry into battle on the edges, the middle would momentarily become one big hole. Moreover, standing in the center of that hole would be Darius himself, conducting affairs from his headquarters in the very heart of the Persian army. Alexander took a calculated risk and kept a portion of his own cavalry back out of the action, hidden in the middle of the Greek forces.

You guessed it. Alexander was right. The instant the hole opened up in the center, he lead his cavalry at full charge, splitting the Persian forces in two, making Darius run for his life. The Persian generals hastily called retreat and their numerous troops fell into chaos and disorder, surrendering as quickly as possible. In three minutes, the whole battle changed.

Tomorrow is Unknown — Anything Can Happen!

Alexander was a great person of hope. He knew that every day is fresh and new, that nothing is impossible, because **anything** can happen. If you have a purpose, you have something valuable to hope for. If you have hope, you can always make plans. If you make plans and do them, anything can happen, including a victory. Even when it looks like you should lose, **you could win.**

That's what history teaches us. In many stories, large and small, there is a theme of hope that runs through the whole course of human existence. When we embrace hope we have what it takes to endure. If we never give in, tomorrow will come and we'll have a fresh start.

Life isn't about self-improvement – **it's about living well.**

So often we are afraid of the unknown. We fear that anything can happen, and we tend to think that those "anythings" are horrible things. Yet your hope provides great courage and strength for the very same reason – **anything can happen.** Hope looks at tomorrow and sees the possibilities for good. Fear looks at tomorrow and sees nothing but lack. Get your eyes off the lack and on to the object of your hope. That is how we turn destiny into a design for living.

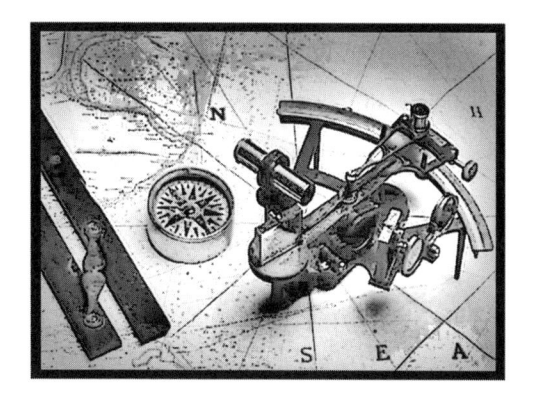

Chapter VI

Cultivate Hope

In which we understand that hope requires attention. It cannot be taken for granted lest it wither. Hope is worth the time and trouble it takes to make it grow.

If all you want is to stay afloat, then even a raft will keep you up out of the water. If your destination is bigger than a little river, you will need to create a vessel that is more sea worthy. How can you do that?

The answer is found in the learning curve: with each trial come better, innovative depths of hope that help you to contain even more hope. It is really true that as we endure the storms and practice the art of sailing through life, we gain skills. We become better navigators, better pilots, and better hope-ers.

When we were children, the tasks that we had to master were small and limited. At the time they seemed quite challenging, but by working at them, we learned and improved. Now that we're older it doesn't take even a lick of thought to brush our teeth, make a bed, or add two plus two, but once upon a time those were big jobs.

Gaining hope is the same. Having hope and preserving it on short voyages creates competency and greater levels of hope. We are able to add to our hope. That is like trading up from a raft to a catboat, and eventually from a catboat to a schooner. You would never presume to cross an ocean on a raft, but in a five-star frigate, you have what it takes.

This principle is very important, especially if your dreams and your purpose in life are distant. It means that you may not have enough hope and skill to get to your dreams today, but by working at "sailing", you will gain the skills and the vessel you need to one day make the crossing. That is good hope indeed.

Hope is Holistic

You see hope is more than just a good feeling. It is the ground out of which spring all the wonders of life:

>Faith
>Patience
>Care
>Charity
>And the "oomph" to keep on going.

When we choose life, anything can happen. We will have influence on the world, and we will live and grow. However, when we choose death, well, dead is dead. That's it. The show's over. That's why the solution to hopelessness isn't death – the solution is to **go get hope**.

At this point, when I talk to groups, someone finally is so frustrated they jump up to let me know that when it comes to them, I am wrong. "Bob, you don't know how crappy my life is. Things are impossible. Nothing will ever change, least of all me. I am hopeless because the situation is really, really bad…and by the way, I don't even like swimming let alone sailing."

They raise an interesting point. I understand their frustration because I know that it takes real energy to go from hopelessness to hopefulness. I usually answer by asking them a question in return.

"Is it easier to have hope when:
1. You've just won the sweepstakes?
2. All your bills are due early but your paycheck is late?
3. You're lost on a lonely road, your car has given up the ghost, no one is in sight, your cell phone is dead, and it looks like its going to rain?"

The correct answer is:
4. All of the above.

It is just as easy to have hope when external things are bad as when externals are good.

Hope is Greater than your Circumstances

Think about it. The last time you were full of hope, did it relate to what was happening, or did it relate to what you had on the inside of you?

Hope is an internal thing. You can have hope or lack hope no matter what your circumstances look like. Having something nice happen to you is nice, but it won't make you hopeless or hopeful, at least not automatically. Truth is, you can have hope in abundance in any and all circumstances. That is because HOPE is not connected to circumstances, externals, events, thoughts, or feelings. Hope is a condition – an anticipation of good, in general.

Hope is a state you exist in. Like saying, "I live in North Dakota" or "I'm in a state of confusion." Even when the particulars are hopeless (as with an incurable disease) hope can prevail. It is anticipating good to come even out of our worst troubles. Even knowing my expectations may not be met, I remain hopeful that some good will occur.

Can you add to hope, become more hopeful? Can you take away from it?

Yes to both.

Hope can be gained, lost, or sustained because it belongs to you. It relates to your attitude and your emotions, but these things do not make your hope; they are cousins and work with hope. Like happiness, hope is a consequence of something else.

Because hope belongs to you, no one can take away your hope; it must be surrendered. In the same way, no one can force hope upon you, it must be accepted.

It seems so very clear to me that hope is always in the possession of the individual. How else does one explain those people who were concentration camp victims, in the most appalling conditions, but were still able to rise above the situation and hold to their hope? How else can one conceive of groups that are so dedicated to their organizational goal that they share a deep and abiding belief they will succeed, even when immediate circumstances aren't favorable to their will?

Friends, in reality, circumstances only have the power we give to them.

The Flower of Hope

My wife, who loves to work in the garden, will tell you that hope is a "cultivar," which means it is a plant that needs tender loving care to grow. It requires looking after. The ground needs to be prepared, the enemies of the plant need to be removed (we call that weeding), and fertilizer and water are required to get the most out of the plant.

Cultivars always produce something wonderful for life. An orange tree produces oranges. Potato plants produce potatoes. We value these plants for their fruits. They nourish and sustain us, and we delight in their differences of taste and texture.

Other cultivars, like roses, produce extraordinary flowers and scents. We may not eat them, but they make life much more enjoyable and beautiful.

Have you noticed that there are other plants that do remarkably well under almost any condition? We call these hardy organisms "weeds." Every summer you can come to North Dakota and visit my house and see for yourself my bumper crop of dandelions. I didn't have to plant a single one of them, yet they come up throughout the yard in abundance.

If I diligently race outside I can mow over them, cutting them down to the nubs. Standing at the street and looking in on my yard, I admire how neat and trim it all looks – totally weed free. Except first thing tomorrow morning, when I glance out the window, you know what I'll see? A thick lush crop of dandelions all over again.

Unless the dandelion is removed at the root, it will continue to grow back, over and over again, stronger each time.

Our Life has to be Weeded to be Productive

Dandelions are not cultivars. They actually take advantage over the Kentucky Blue Grass that I'm trying to grow. Weeds are vicious competitors. They steal water, they steal land space, they steal nourishment, and they spread themselves out high and wide, stealing sunlight. There's not much left for the cultivars when weeds have been allowed to grow free and clear.

My life has many similarities to my yard – it is a curious and competitive blend of cultivars and weeds, of the beautiful and the ugly, the useful and useless. No matter how often I take a lawn mower to my life, vowing to change every behavior and belief that I don't value, when I get up the next morning, there they all are, grinning at me, growing stronger. Somehow in life, just like in the lawn, I have to deal with the roots of things, not just the heads.

Hope is a Cultivar

Hope is a cultivar. I want to grow it and enjoy it, and have more of it every season. It takes grooming to get that to happen. It doesn't grow overnight; it needs weeding and watering and feeding to make it strong and stable.

Just like in the garden, once the cultivars have established themselves they don't require much maintenance, but to get them started and healthy, you have to apply a lot of "science" and "labor."

They aren't as easy to grow as weeds; however, you can't eat weeds. Weeds don't just hurt cultivars; **they hurt us** because they don't contribute fruit or delight. They are enemies to the very things that we need and want, which make them our enemies, personally.

Enemies are Against You – Hope is For You

Do I sound neutral about weeds? No way! I hate them. I hate the weeds in my life, too. Being lukewarm about weeds is no way to win the battle against them. They are my enemies, and frankly, I don't ever want to put up with them willingly.

A lot of people don't like to talk about enemies. They feel that is way too aggressive and confrontational. "It's not nice to hate our enemies." Let me assure you that **people are not your enemies**. The enemies in life are the "weeds" that are contrary to your purpose.

If your purpose is to help people, then apathy is your enemy. If your purpose is to build something, then laziness is your enemy. If your purpose is to learn something, then ignorance is your enemy.

Granted, other people may be apathetic, lazy, or ignorant, but those people are not your enemy. It is their motivation (or lack of motivation), THAT is the enemy.

I used to think it wasn't "nice" to hate anything. Nevertheless, as I have aged (and matured) I have seen some really awful things in this world. I have seen cruelty, and bigotry, and hard-heartedness. Those are wicked and hateful. They are worthy of my hatred and disdain. I can't accomplish my goal or raise up my standard of hope if I entertain cruel, bigoted, or hard-hearted thoughts and deeds. They get in the way of the very things that I desperately want to succeed in.

Go Ahead – Hate the Enemy!

If I don't hate them with real hatred, then I find that I tolerate them. I may assign them a lesser status, or simply try to put them out of sight and out of mind, but the reality is, unless they are dealt with in the same way I'd deal with a weed, they are sucking life out of my hope. They are stealing the water, nourishment and sunshine that rightly belong to me.

When other people get in my way with bigotry, or cruelty, or hardhearts, I deal with the weeds and work quickly to forgive them.

People are never the problem. If we give ourselves the luxury to think that people are the problem, then the simple solution is to get rid of the people. I believe the Nazi's tried that and they called it the "final solution."

Therefore I make it my business to feed my hope with the truth. Truth acts as fertilizer and water. It feeds me on the inside. Whenever I embrace the truth and work to believe it, I find that I am more buoyant – better able to float through the circumstances of daily living.

I also make it my business to weed my personal garden. I will not tolerate the things that are contrary to my purpose. Make no mistake; this is sometimes very hard work, because there are many selfish and competing beliefs that live inside me.

I have to diligently come against the thoughts and deeds that run contrary to my aim. If I find that I am thinking wrong thoughts, I have to stop what I'm doing and insert a truthful set of principles to think about. If I am talking improperly, I have to stop it right away, and then make sure that I speak out the truth – that I speak out my desire and my hope, in positive honest terms.

I don't weed my life everyday. There are many things that occupy my time, and constant weeding isn't necessary. However, when those

Chapter 6: Cultivate Hope

dandelions start to show their little yellow heads, it's time to go for the roots and be done with them.

Life isn't about self-improvement - **it's about living well.**

The goal of life isn't punishment; it is to enjoy our life. Hope grows when we cultivate it. Hope grows when we aim to have hope and make good choices. Hope grows when we protect it from its enemies, and when we feed it the truth. It's really very simple, as long as you want hope.

> *The goal of life isn't punishment; it is to enjoy our life. Hope grows when we cultivate it.*

Chapter VII

Natural Hope

In which hope and wishing are contrasted and we learn that hope is full of promise. Because hope is part of the human condition, it is subject to natural laws. Hope is involved in the "give and take" of energy. Remove the obstacles to hope.

There is an old nursery rhyme that states "If wishes were horses then beggars would ride." Which is to say, that beggars make idle wishes but won't do what's necessary to get a ride.

In my house we've simplified it to, "If wishes were fishes then they would be fried."

Hope is used very loosely in contemporary English. When we say, "I hope the Vikings win the Super Bowl," (or as my wife would say, "the World Series") we usually mean no more and no less than, "I WISH they'd win."

But **wishing and hoping are really two different things**.

A wish may be a dream your heart makes, and you can wish upon a star, but a wish is disconnected. Wishes are idle – they don't do anything nor do they motivate action. Wishes are altogether absent of desire, passion, and compassion.

Hope is materially different. It involves more than the thing you hope for; it is an investment made by the one who hopes. It becomes an extension of the self – a leaning out into the future with a decided will for good. Hope is an internal state of anticipation. Therefore hope is personal.

Wishing won't get you there

We don't (and won't) work for what we wish for. However, when we hope for something, we tap into our personal resources in order to create the good outcome we want.

Scientists who sit in front of their test tubes, thinking, "I wish someone would find a cure for cancer," are useless compared to those who **hope** to find the cure. Scientists who hope to find the cure are actually looking for it. We know they are in action. They are running experiments and thinking about the possible solutions night and day. Hope works like that in our common everyday lives too. When we have hope, we find that we have the motive for action.

> *Scientists who sit in front of their test tubes, thinking, "I wish someone would find a cure for cancer," are useless compared to those who* **hope** *to find the cure.*

Hope doesn't exist in a vacuum. Wishing may be disconnected, but hope is inside the soul of people. It is a living thing because we are living things. Like all living things, hope is subject to natural laws, because we are subject to natural laws.

(It's time to dust off your science textbooks and do some review. Remember Sir Isaac Newton, the guy who was hit by an apple and suddenly invented the law of gravity? He didn't stop there. The more he and other scientists looked at the order of nature, the more fundamental laws they uncovered. We're going to take a detour and look at a couple of them. If you aren't into science, now is a good time to bake a pie and make some coffee.)

Inertia: A Law of Motion

Let us first inspect Newton's law of motion called inertia. The principle can be stated like this: an object at rest will tend to stay at rest, and an object in motion will tend to stay in motion. It takes outside energy to alter the present motion.

Anyone who's ridden a bicycle has experienced inertia first hand. When you begin to mount the bike, it has to be held in place or it will simply fall to the ground. The bike is "at rest" and wants to stay that way. To get it going you have to give the pedals a strong, deliberate push, and follow that push-off with a number of pedal strokes. What you are doing is overcoming inertia, getting that bike into a new state of motion. It takes extra energy to do that.

Once the bike is up and running it is really easy to keep it that way. Now inertia is working for you. The bike stays balanced up and down, and you don't need to pedal so hard to keep it rolling. Life is a dream and you have the principle of inertia to thank for it ... until you suddenly see the motor bus bearing down at thirty miles an hour. Now you have to battle inertia in order to get that bike into a state of rest before you are resting underneath the bus,

(proving Newton's other law that for every action there is an equal and opposite reaction)

Bicycles, Water Pitchers, and Hope

I think I can already hear some of you thinking, "What on earth does that have to do with hope? You don't ride hope like a bicycle."

Since we are living things and are subject to inertia, so is the hope that resides within us. Hope that is seldom used is "at rest", and it takes real energy to get that hope up and running. Like the bicycle, once we use our hope, it takes less energy to maintain it. It wants to work on our behalf. The more we hope the more hope we have to hope with. (I don't just hope so; I know so, by practical experience in my own life, as well as by observation of the world.)

I use the following exercise to highlight how inertia works in individuals and groups:

> *Imagine a pitcher of water sitting in the middle of a table. You want to lift it up but can't. Invent as many reasons as you can to explain why you can't overcome inertia.*

This usually generates a list that includes items like:

- Can't reach it
- Not strong enough to lift it
- Am blind and can't see it to move it
- Don't know how to move it
- Don't have permission to move it
- Don't want to move it
- Someone has glued it to the table

Things that limit us: Physical Barriers

As you can see, the first three items are physical limitations. It is an important truth that we can and will face tasks that are beyond our physical ability to overcome.

Sometimes, in order to solve a problem we need to look at things from a different angle, creating new processes in order to make it work. We may have to modify the work or the tools by providing supplemental assistance. The whole idea behind the Americans with Disabilities Act is that organizations have to find creative solutions when employees and customers have physical limitations.

I am not aware of a physical deterrent to hope. Perhaps there is a medical condition that will not allow the human will to express itself. Certainly there are types of depression which seem to be chemical problems on the structural level of the brain and have very little to do with the soul of the individual. In cases like that, one can receive supplemental assistance by taking appropriate medications. That is a good solution to bipolar depression.

The remaining items on our list have nothing to do with physical limitations. They demonstrate factors related to our humanity.

Things that limit us: Lack of Knowledge

A person can be hired to do something they are physically capable of performing, yet lack the knowledge – the "know how" - to accomplish the tasks. If lack of knowledge is the problem, then the solution isn't to beat on the person or to fire them, it is to get them trained and educated.

I remember many years ago being so frustrated with a worker who "refused" to pull his weight on our project. Then I discovered that he could hardly read. The problem wasn't (as I first thought) that he was a bad person; the problem was that he didn't know what to do until it was told to him verbally.

How many times do we face problems (individually or in the work place) when the real solution is to **learn** something? I believe your reading this book can be a learning solution for you. It is entirely possible that others have gone for most of their lives without any idea of what it takes to live a more satisfying life. They aren't bad people; they just need to learn. It's a true statement that you can't know what you don't know.

Things that limit us: Lack of Permission

I really like it when people identify "permission" as an inertia problem. I think there are many times when we'd like to make a decision or take action, but we falter because we are not sure that we have permission to do it. One fellow I know told me that his solution to this problem is to ALWAYS do what he wants to do, because "it is easier to get forgiveness than it is to get permission."

I have known others whose mother or father used "permission" as a tool of control. When they grow up and are out on their own, they still rarely feel that they "should" do whatever it is they'd like to do. They are constantly nagged by the lack of permission. That is a real pickle. Some counseling is very helpful in situations like that. It takes a consistent, vigorous application of truth to help free them. They need to hear the truth, believe it, and apply it. The permission that really counts is what we give ourselves as we pursue our purpose. Sometimes that's easier to say than it is to "feel," but that doesn't change the truth of it.

In a work situation where a problem seems intractable and people just don't seem to want to come up with fresh solutions, the inertia is more than likely caused by a lack of permission. Therefore, give them permission to try something new – oh yes, and give them permission to try and fail. When the leadership gives permission, sometimes that is all that's necessary to release people to perform.

Things that limit us: Lack of Desire

Likewise, the inertia that comes from apathy – the lack of desire – is a profound problem. When we **don't want** to do something, it takes a great deal of external energy to force us to do it.

The phenomenon of "learned helplessness" comes into play here. We may not want to do something because we believe it is utterly useless to try. If our conclusion about our life learning is that we CAN'T do something, then we will not WANT to do it either. If we believe that working on our hope is too much effort with too little pay-off, we give up the desire to do anything about it. Our hope dwindles and we freeze in time. In order to stimulate action you have to want to make changes.

Making people WANT something is dicey business. We have all tried forcing people, and we've tried enticing them, and we've tried commanding them, and we've tried ignoring them. Most of the time, these did not overcome the inertia. Somehow what's required is that they have to discover that they want it on their own. Therefore, you can encourage them and lay out the many benefits of making a change, but if they refuse, you will ultimately have to go on ahead without them.

Things that limit us: Our Enemies

Finally, the last item on the list "someone has glued the pitcher to the table" is similar to facing an enemy of our hope. Something is sabotaging the system. (Notice, I did not say "someone" is sabotaging the system, even though I know that resistance and undermining come through other human beings; PEOPLE ARE NOT OUR ENEMY. Wrong beliefs and wrong motives are the enemy.)

When you know you are trying to do the right thing in the right way, but something seems to be in the way, when inertia won't allow you to accomplish what should otherwise work – there may well be an enemy at work.

In the same way that you'd have to use glue remover to free the pitcher, you may well have to deal with the thing that is in your way. Deming, the management philosopher, would probably consider overcoming this type of inertia the step of "Removing Obstacles to Quality." I simply consider it, "Dealing with the weeds."

For example, if your selfishness has you more concerned with making sure you are "taken care of" than accomplishing your mission, you will have to weed it out. You do this by taking deliberate action that is contrary to your fears as well as by examining what you really believe (so that you can deal with the roots of those fears by replacing them with positive truths that you need on the inside of you).

Inertia is a good model for stimulating change because it helps us remember that there are many reasons, good and bad, why some things don't work. Don't toss in the towel because something is hard. Just remind yourself that inertia is at play, and use the inertia model to help you figure out what you need to do to overcome it.

Entropy: An Inescapable Law

There is another natural law at work in us. It springs from the fact that all of the cosmos is a finite, created system. That law is the unfailing second law of thermodynamics: entropy. Entropy is the natural law that everything wears out. Things in order go to disorder. Organized go to disorganized. Everything falls apart into chaos and runs out of steam. It's impossible to have perpetual motion and it's impossible to escape death without some outside energy being introduced into the system to counteract entropy. Entropy teaches us that energy must come IN to the system to keep the system going, and that it takes energy to establish and maintain organization or things won't hold together.

We know this to be true in so many ways. We go for a walk in the woods. There by the path we spy a dead tree, fallen over and bleaching under the sun. Entropy is hard at work – even the tree has worn out. It no longer has an internal organizing principle. There is no life force to keep one cell working with another. Without organization, the same forces that once fed the tree are working to disintegrate it to rubbish status – little disorganized atomic pieces (which will also eventually unbundle and shed their energy).

Such a cheery thought.

Nothing left to itself will remain. Everything is either falling into chaos, or it is working to counteract destruction. There is no middle road. Eventually, everything wears out without an infusion of energy.

This is true for people and for people systems. Without some kind of energy coming in from the outside and without some attention to the functioning of the person or organization, entropy is fast about us and the good things disintegrate.

The Acceptable Level of Mediocrity

I have what I call the theory of "the acceptable level of mediocrity." It takes into account the reality of entropy. The theory states that unless someone is consciously choosing a high standard (and doing what it takes to make that high standard a reality), things will run downhill to a state of mediocrity. Because the mediocre is "almost good," people are willing to put up with it for quite a while. If things get too bad, then folks become grossly uncomfortable and that spurs them to some kind of action. The system gets charged up for a while, but it only receives enough energy to get back to the acceptable state of mediocrity. Once things are happily mediocre, the energy to change dissolves, and everything will run downhill again.

When is the right time to make a declaration? Do we declare something after it has been done, or do we make a declaration before we've started?

This is true for individuals and for groups. If you need something more than the mediocre, you will have to apply some energy. You'll have to declare what quality workmanship is, hold everyone's feet to the fire, and do whatever is necessary to make sure quality happens. In a business, this outside energy could be a boss, or a co-worker who really cares, or customers who insist on the best – or it might even be you!

It takes Energy to be More than Mediocre

In your own life the decision to actually enjoy living has to come from YOU. Don't wait for a significant other to motivate you (in the real world we call that 'nagging'). Your solution starts with YOU.

The only way to fight entropy – to be more than mediocre – is to choose to get the energy you need and to organize and use the energy you have.

I know that sounds like work.

I'm not sorry about that. It takes work to have quality. Quality means you have to pay attention to what you are planning, thinking, saying, and doing. Life has to be more than 8 hours of sleep, 12 hours of television, 3 hours of eating, and 1 measly hour of productivity. Living that kind of life will always leave you coming up short. The best you will ever have is an acceptable level of mediocrity, where things aren't horrible, but they sure aren't good either. It takes great living to have a great life.

Hope is part of that process. When we declare that we will live a hopeful life, we are taking deliberate action to fight entropy. As long as we're alive, we aim toward the kind of satisfaction and happiness that most people never get to experience, because they won't pay the price of admission.

Hope Starts with a Declaration

This raises an interesting point. When is the right time to make a declaration? Do we declare something after it has been done, or do we make a declaration before we've started?

The Declaration of Independence was written before the Revolutionary War started. In fact, if the people hadn't organized and made the decision to create a new country with its own rule, they would never have needed to write the Declaration. Without the Declaration, there would never have been a need to fight the war to establish the Independence they knew they must achieve.

Any significant action begins by making a declaration. "I declare that I will live a life full of hope." The time to make that noble claim isn't when you are so full of hope you're busting at the seams; it is when you are beat up, dragged out, and empty. You rise and look at your life and make the decision: "I will be a person of hope. I will have a quality life." Until you declare something, entropy will be working against you, and inertia will be happily holding you in place.

Like a ship at sea, the elements will take their toll. You will need to scrape some barnacles off your life, now and again, and splash on some fresh paint. Maintaining your life is worth every effort that you give it. Darn few people will waltz by and say, "Gosh, you look like you could use a good scrubbing," and then fix you up. I'm not saying it can't happen, I'm just saying that it is YOUR LIFE. Therefore it's up to YOU to make the most of living.

Life is not about self-improvement – **it's about living well.**

Even natural, physical laws show us that quality living requires attention to quality. You can do that. Even if you've never been a person of hope, you can stand up today and make your own Declaration of Independence. Believe me, it is worth it.

Chapter VIII

Invest the Best

In which we apply three principles of investment to maximize the hope that we hold inside.

Hope is an investment. When you build your hope, you are making an investment for your future. Like any investment, you can't see the end from the beginning, but you know eventually it will work to your benefit.

The Rule of 72

When people invest money, they talk about the Rule of 72. The Rule of 72 says that when you invest $1 at 1% interest, because of the principle of compounding interest, in 72 years your dollar will double.

Now I'm not a math whiz, but I know enough to sharpen my pencil and take a hard look at how this can work for me.

According to the Rule of 72, if I invest that same dollar at 6% interest, my dollar will double in 12 years. So, for a small increase of only 5% in the interest rate, my waiting time has come down by 60 years.

If I invest that dollar at 10% interest, it will double every 7 years 2½ months. In 21½ years, that little dollar will have turned into $8, cold hard cash.

That's the power of investing with compound interest.

I believe the same kind of principle is at work when we invest in our soul. As we increase, we are not simply adding hope to our lives, we are investing it – it is compounding! The longer we leave it to work, the more work it does. The higher the interest rate, the faster it will double itself.

> *...we are not simply adding hope to our lives, we are investing it – it is compounding!*

I think there are some simple ways to invest hope. Like any good investment counselor, I'll advise you to put your eggs in a few different baskets. Here are three of them that you can use.

First, invest some of your own hope in others.

Share the hope that you have. When we give to others we may think we are "giving something away for nothing," but what we're really doing is investing in them. If I can take some of my hope and impart it to others, then I have made an investment in their lives. As they prosper, I prosper indirectly. Hope from any source at any time is a good thing.

Yet there is a direct benefit. Heaven knows you can't force hope on people any more than you can force medicine or food. Yet it is yours to offer. The very act of making the offer creates space in your soul for expansion. Hope that is given actually creates more and deeper hope in the giver.

Priming the Pump

There's natural evidence of how this works. For me I just go to the example of Grandpa's old well. When we were kids, we loved to go visit Grandpa. His house and yard were totally different than our normal urban environment. For one thing, he kept chickens in the yard and if we wanted eggs for breakfast, we had to go and try to get some out from under those noisy, nasty hens – and they didn't appreciate our groping little hands. And the rooster? There is no meaner or more arrogant creature in the animal kingdom than a rooster.

> *In the country, Grandpa and his well had never heard of "instant on." If you wanted water, you had to pump for it.*

He also had a well, with an old pump on the top of it. We'd be running around outside, having fun (trying to escape that miserable rooster) and we'd get so thirsty. Since we weren't supposed to run in and out of the house, it meant we had to go to the well.

In the city, we were "instant on" kids. If we wanted anything we could get it instantly. Want ice? Go to the freezer and get some. Want water? Turn a faucet and immediately you have more water than you know what to do with.

In the country, Grandpa and his well had never heard of "instant on." If you wanted water, you had to pump for it. I mean, you *really* had to pump for it. One or two pushes on the lever handle weren't going to satisfy you. You had to work for your water and pump like mad.

What I didn't know then was that every time I got water from the well, I was putting science into motion. By pumping the handle, I was creating a need, a space that something had to fill. All my furious pumping was forming an imbalance in pressure, and nature abhors an imbalance. Because the pump was connected to underground water that meant it began to call water up the pipe until finally it would gush out in tremendous fat bursts with each draw.

Hope is like that. When you give it to someone, you are pumping out of your own soul, creating a need, a space. Since hope is foundational to quality living, as you share hope, you draw up new, fresh hope for yourself. It may take a little time and effort (just like Grandpa's well), but when you get it going it is more than enough for you and anyone else who happens to be nearby. You'll all get soaked with hope.

Second, investments take patience.

Ooh, don't you just hate the "P" word sometimes? An investment, by its very definition, is an allocation of money (or other resources) *over time* that will bring an increase. Farmers invest seed by banking it in the ground. They have to wait an entire growing season before they can reap the full results of their work. If they were to "peek", they would kill the very plants that they are trying to grow. If they became impatient, they would harvest the fruits before they are ripe and ready. Farmers have to learn patience because plants need time to mature.

Patience is a Virtue

We would do well to take a tip from the farmers. Our maturity, our growing and living processes, take time. We may hear a word of truth and appropriate it in a single moment, but it takes real time before that truth has established itself, before we have learned to live with it on the whole.

Look at this from a different perspective. If we always got exactly what we thought we wanted the very moment that we wanted it, we'd have married that snotty nosed kid we had such a crush on in Junior High (and divorced by age 16). In my case I'd have a closet full of Nehru jackets, bell bottoms, and clogs (don't ask me why I thought they were cool). We'd have spent all of our resources on toys that break, relationships that were shallow, and candy instead of real food.

If we always got exactly what we thought we wanted the very moment that we wanted it, we'd have married that snotty nosed kid we had such a crush on in Junior High...

Even when we are passionate about what we want, having it denied or delayed actually enhances our enjoyment of the experience, and helps us focus on what we really want. There is nothing bad about wanting something. A quality life is full of patience. We know that good things are worth waiting for, and maintaining our passion over time helps us shake out the bad things along the way.

Let Time do its Work

Time allows our hope to focus itself more keenly where we truly want to invest it. Our vision matures and changes. Our needs grow and change. Even the outside world around us changes. In the same manner, the object of our hope will change. Hope itself is unchangeable since hope is a condition, but the expression of that hope requires time in order to be perfected.

You can't rush quality any more than you can rush a growing season or the interest rate at your local bank. So don't be in such an all-fired hurry. Understand that your hope will take time, and that this is a good thing.

Third, investment requires connection to something greater than oneself. Invest in something bigger than you.

In the natural realm this means that we invest in something beyond our own mattress – we put our money to work in CD's or Mutual Funds, or send our kids to college (investing in their future), or we begin businesses or take new jobs. In the case of hope we need to bank our life with something that is larger than our own gumption or brains. We need God.

A Good Example

In Alcoholics Anonymous, there is what is called the 12-step program. By working through these steps, individuals can gain the help they need to put addiction in its place and to liberate themselves to live in a new freedom. One of the steps is to acknowledge and call upon a "Higher Power." It is not my intention to use this as a vehicle for any specific proselytizing, but I know this truth through observation and personal experience: hope and faith are intimate friends.

Our point of view will always be limited because we are finite limited created beings. When we are consciously connected to something greater, more powerful, more right, and more kind than our individual self and expectations, we are in the right place to grow. Without acknowledging and connecting to something greater than oneself, to God, we have only the self to hang on to, which is rather like being in the water without even a life vest to hang on to.

Since investment means placing our own limited valuable resources in the hands of some other person or company, in the same fashion we need to invest our hope with our God. Face facts, none of us is the "be all and the end all" of the world. If we don't know whether a Higher Power exists or not, can we at least agree that we aren't It? Therefore, turn the larger issues of life over to God and let your hope grow and multiply.

> *When we are consciously connected to something greater, more powerful, more right, and more kind than our individual self and expectations, we are in the right place to grow.*

Investing in Hope Always Pays

Hope is a lot like an investment because by its very nature, hope looks forward. As the song says, we may "look behind from where we've come," but our hope exclusively looks forward. It anticipates, and we are lifted up by the promise of greater things.

Winners are people of hope. A real winner enjoys life and has great capacity for hope. Winners are optimistic about their own future, even if the future of the world looks bleak. They anticipate good outcomes and they organize their lives to make them happen.

Winners are Ordinary People of Extraordinary Hope

A great sorrow in America is that we think winners wear Super Bowl rings. If we haven't broken a world record or had a TV special written about us, we feel like failures. In truth, the real winners of life are the ordinary people who rise to the challenge of every day, go to sleep, and rise again.

It's not the set backs that count, it's not how many falls you've suffered, it's not the rejections or the accolades; it's all the times you've picked yourself up from the floor, dusted off your clothes, and pressed ahead once again.

I think life is very tough for most of us. Having falls is a natural consequence because life is risky, and every risk isn't going to pan out. You'll have difficulties. However, if you are willing to try again, then the path of your life is like a staircase. You may fall, but every time you get up again, you are on a step higher than when you began.

Life isn't about self-improvement – **it's about living well.**

Growing hope in others prospers the hope that you seek to grow in yourself. Hope is an investment, and like any investment, it takes time. So make your deposit, trust the process, and get the Rule of 72 working for your soul.

Chapter IX

Who Are You?

> In which we examine the role of our identity. We are defined by who we are, not by our works. A definite identity is a valuable asset because it relates to our purpose and the promise of hope.

You can't steer a boat unless it is in motion. Where there is no movement or impulse of any kind, the rudder is useless. When a boat is moving, even if it is going the exact wrong direction, the rudder is an excellent tool for correction. Although it may be the smallest part of the sailing craft, from stem to stern the boat will obey its will.

People of hope are people in motion. Though they do not control their environment, their society, or their families, people of hope acknowledge that they are free, free to control themselves and to make choices and changes. Therefore, when things go wrong or they feel that they are adrift, they don't measure their security by their assessment of their own strength or bank accounts. They take their security from knowing that there is a tomorrow and that they can make good choices to get from here to there. They do not focus on what they lack; rather they tend to focus on who they are. They are led by their purpose in life.

Where are you going?

Are you dismayed right now because you are going somewhere you don't want to go? There are five reasons that I can think of for that to happen.

1. First, you are in the middle of a storm, where the wind and waves are over-powering. In such a circumstance, the rudder and the rest of the ship are no match for the violence of the environment. Once the storm has abated, you can again hoist your sails and use your rudder to make course corrections and get you back on line.

2. The second situation is similar, but instead of being over-powered by your environment, you have given control to someone else. When you tie your ship to another that is stronger, you have no control over your direction. You have to endure the trip or else sever the connection. As long as you are tethered, your direction is subordinate to theirs.

3. Third, you have deliberately chosen to "tack" across the wind. In such a situation you have chosen a direction based on its long term merits, not its short term advantages. When you tack, you may have to make changes and choices that are not pleasant, but you do so because you believe it is best in the long run. It takes real wisdom to lay aside your short term comfort in order to gain your long term victory. It has always been thus for sailors. What sustains us is the certain knowledge that the ultimate aim is worth the effort; that we are doing the best today to position our tomorrow.

4. The fourth reason is a tough one. Simply put, **you** refuse to make the necessary changes to go a different way. You may profess intellectually that you want to head in a different direction, but it is your own hand, firmly gripping the tiller that commands the rudder. A good life, like good sailing, requires a clear assessment of our choices and changes. Good words and good intentions are fine, but let's not fool ourselves. We are fully capable of being dishonest. We need to watch what we are really doing and then make changes based on the results that we see.

5. Finally, the fifth reason (a rather common one I suspect) is that you lack a centerboard or keel. When sailing, the rudder is able to make changes in direction because the keel of the boat is doing its job, biting into the water, creating a forward thrust and stability. When the rudder is turned at the back of the boat, it parts the water unevenly, and the boat turns trying to re-establish equilibrium. Without a keel, the boat is not connected to the water.

    Imagine trying to steer a floating cork with a rudder. Because the cork has no "bite" it only skims the surface; it cannot productively use its natural buoyancy. It bobs here and there and is helplessly driven by currents of water and wind. In such a situation, the rudder lacks meaning and ability because the vessel has no definition.

Finding an answer to the question, "Who are you?" is very important, because our identity is our keel.

The Power of Purpose

It never ceases to amaze me as to how people define themselves. In the United States, when you are introduced to somebody, it is simply enough to state your name and occupation. "Hello, I'm Bob. I'm a consultant."

> *If you identify yourself by your circumstances, then your circumstances control your life...*

Now think about it. What does that really tell you about me (other than the fact that I can't get a steady job like everybody else)? Why are we defining ourselves by our job titles? In truth we are not our jobs. Our jobs are simply things we do and get paid for doing. Knowing what I do for a living doesn't give you any indication who I am as a person.

Where do you find your identity? If you identify yourself by your circumstances, then your circumstances control your life – **you** don't. You have sacrificed the freedom that you have by giving yourself a definition based on something that is happening to you. Your circumstances have nothing to do with the "who" that you are. Let's take a moment and look at this truth. You are **not** your circumstances. They do not define you because they are not YOU. YOU are YOU.

So what if your current circumstances are your own fault? What if you shoplifted a loaf of bread and now the entire metropolitan police force has surrounded the house and a SWAT team is assembling on the front lawn? OK, you deserve it. But the circumstances don't define you. The WHO that you are is separate from the WHAT that you have done. My advice is to pay the price for the crime and learn quickly that you are free to be someone who makes much better choices, starting today and lasting well into the future.

I was at the grocery store the other day. I don't know if you're like me, but I can't pick the fast checkout line no matter how hard I try. I mean, here was a lady with three items, while in the next line was a guy buying two carts worth of canned foods. I quickly beat about 20 other people to the short line. What I didn't know was that this nice lady in front of me was going to buy her few items with a credit card, using the brand new "self service machine," something she had never done before in her life.

So here I was, trapped behind the learning curve once again (HER learning curve) and I had this excellent opportunity to practice patience, while I watched the other line moving swiftly like a NASCAR semi-final! Having nothing better to do to occupy my time I listened to the folks around me. I heard the little cashier (a young woman I have known for 11 years) say to the credit card lady, "Well, as a new mother I wouldn't know how to operate those cause I don't have any credit cards yet."

As they waited for the transaction to complete (for the fifth time) she bagged the few items and commented, "Well, as a new mother I know how important calcium is to your diet."

Finally, it's my turn and she turns to me sweetly and says, "Hi Bob. How you feeling?"

"Wonderful!"

"That's good, cause being a new mother I'm sure not getting the sleep I should be, but that's to be expected I guess."

It was easy to see that since the birth of her child, this lady had acquired a significant piece of her identity. She wasn't Jane Doe, Cashier, anymore. She was a MOTHER. Although I am sincerely happy about her family situation (after all, children are a blessing – no matter how it may seem), I was also sad to think that for most of her life she had been lacking a vital component of a quality life: a positive identity.

It got me thinking about identity. Not only how we tend to identify ourselves, but also where our identity ought to come from. What is its natural source?

It's not what you know; it's who you are.
I believe that in western culture, men and women usually identify themselves in the following ways:

- **What we do**
  (Our job...Our roles)
- **Who we know**
- **What we own**

When these elements make up our self-definition, we run the risk of having "slippery" identities. I think all of us can relate to the experience I call: When Worlds Collide! This happens when we have multiple identities – a separate identity to go with each role and job.

For instance, let's say my identity at work is "one of the boys", (a jolly joker, able to swear like the best of them, and expert at hanging out at the water cooler). At home I have a different identity in my role as "father" (where I'm the bossy, unsatisfied, nagging Daddy whose children just can't seem to get anything right no matter how angry I get). However at church on a Sunday morning, I greet everyone "just so" and make sure they are seated properly (in as holy a manner as possible) as I do my job of ushering.

Then the worlds collide! I pull into the grocery store, yelling at my kids in the car, and as I jump out the door, red-faced and twitching, a group of buddies from work suddenly walk up to me. Just as I'm grinding my gears, trying to switch my identity, the Pastor from church pulls in and walks right up to the group of us and shakes my hand. Meanwhile, my children just sit in the car, smiling, watching the smoke pour from my ears while my brain does 180's trying to figure out who I'm supposed to be and how I'm supposed to act.

You see there is a deadly problem when we let our jobs and our roles define us. We are selling away our freedom to be true to who we are, and we pay a price for it.

Now I'm not suggesting that if you're crabby at home you should be crabby everywhere else. No one would admire that kind of consistency. What I want to demonstrate is that our possessions and toys, the people that we know, or the jobs and roles we have, are not WHO we are. They are at best manifestations of who we are.

If our job defines us, then we are embarrassed when we introduce ourselves as "Bob, the dishwasher." Alternately, we think too highly of ourselves when we say, "I'm Bob, the CEO." One of the tricks of a high quality life is the comfort of knowing who you are, and being free in that knowledge. In reality, **you are free** from the expectations that others might force upon you, and you are free to express yourself honestly based on your true identity. Remember, freedom always means "free from" and "free to".

As long as our identity is described and proscribed by our roles and other external factors, then our identity doesn't belong to us. And as long as our identity belongs to someone or something other than our self, we lack self-control and have surrendered our life from a "who" to a "what."

A Definite Identity is a Definite Advantage

There is a strange security that some find in refusing to have a set identity. They believe it keeps them from being offensive because they never take on any characteristic that is "definite." By remaining wishy-washy or refusing to have an opinion or trait of their own, they think others will like them better.

Avoiding conflict by never exposing who we really are is a terrible way to live. The sad fact is that somebody somewhere at sometime WILL NOT LIKE YOU. (After all, you don't like everybody *you* meet, why should you expect that everyone else should have to like you?) Even if you avoid being a real person, I guarantee you that there will be more people who will dislike you because you are "phony" than there are those who hate you because you are "definite."

It isn't too late to rise to a new level of identity, one that goes beyond what you do, what you have, or who you know, to an identity that is rooted in the very thing that is special to you: your PURPOSE.

In the best families (and I realize most of us did not have ideal families), our identity springs from the fact that we are loved unconditionally. Our folks and our siblings just plain **love us because we ARE**, not because of what we do. That sets such an important stage for our self-definition. We can easily enjoy our unique personality and purpose. Once we know we are loved for who we are, then we freely build on that foundation. That is why our purpose in life is key to our understanding of who we are.

Our Unique Mission

I believe that people of hope have discovered the power of their freedom. They turn for their identity to their unique purpose. They derive their hope from their vision. They look not so much at what they have or what they can do, as they look at what they want to accomplish, at the outcomes they want to achieve, the purpose of their life – the natural expression of their identity.

> *...people of hope have discovered the power of their freedom.*

What's uniquely powerful about purpose is that even when you lack the very results you most desire you don't lose hope. You still push on toward your aspirations with vigor and determination, because you are looking beyond the struggles of today toward the excellence of tomorrow.

That's another reason why stress has such a hard time stealing from the hopeful. Stress can point out all of today's bad problems and difficult changes, and remind you of all your failed yesterdays, but hope is already looking ahead to tomorrow. (It's like tacking into the wind, the success of the day is measured by the forward progress, not by the particular direction.)

When you build your identity on your purpose – the aim of your life – you are building from the inside out. You are taking the things that are YOU and using them to express yourself to the world.

I have a cousin who, when he was 8 years old, announced to his family one day; "I'm going to be a doctor." Guess what, he became one. That was obviously a powerful vision to him. However, when I talk about our purpose, I'm not talking about job titles.

Our purpose is more often expressed in a general way. Often it sounds like the voice of a child: "I want to help people." "I want to play pretend." "I want to know everything." "What's under every rock?"

Sometimes, as adults, we hear those little child voices inside of us and we get embarrassed. "How foolish," we think. "I am all grown up now and much more sophisticated than that. I certainly don't want anyone to know that all I want is to be helpful."

If we'd quit being ashamed of the simple, childlike parts of us, we'd learn great truths about who we really are. Those little child voices are the early expressions of our purpose in life. As adults we can get our undies in a bundle just trying to sort out "Who am I? Why am I? What am I supposed to do?"

Nevertheless, when we were kids we didn't have any trouble recognizing the things that "turned us on." We just knew we liked some things better than others, and we were naturally drawn to them. Those early attractions are great indicators of our purpose.

Everyone has a Purpose and to Everything there is a Season

I believe that every single human being (regardless of brainpower, maturity, emotional state, or physical stature) has a purpose for being. We're here for a reason, and as we fulfill that purpose, we find that we are satisfying the deepest parts of us.

That's something you can hang your hope on, isn't it?

Having a purpose is broader than having a plan. Plans are narrow in focus. We make plans daily, weekly, annually so that we can live out our purpose. That's why our purpose is expressed in general terms, and why we can stand with a whole group of people who have a similar purpose to our own, and yet discover we are each expressing it in special, individual ways. Plans naturally flow out of our purpose; it's harder trying to find our purpose in the midst of our many plans.

Having a purpose is broader than having a plan. Plans are narrow in focus.

Since our purpose is central to who we are as people, it is central to our identity. It's liberating when we begin saying "Hello, I'm Bob. I like making things," rather than "I'm Bob, the cement guy." It is more revealing as to who we are, isn't it? Perhaps that's a scary thought that somebody would really know what I'm like? Nevertheless, it's also exhilarating – we are moving on the cutting edge of who we are, and it all starts just by declaring it openly.

Personal Mission Statements

If this sounds a bit like writing a mission statement for a corporation, it is. Only this is more important, because organizations are made of individuals. Therefore, the mission statement of each individual is far more meaningful than the corporate mission statement, because it takes quality people, living quality lives, to create uncommon, quality workplaces.

Now, if we can see the value of having a good mission statement in an organization, can't we see its value in our home or our heart? In fact, my best advice is to make some time and write down the very things that are deepest to your core.

Write them down and put them someplace special where you can review them. Don't share them with very many people. They are special to you and should only be opened for discussion among the rare few you consider exceptional. Begin by treasuring them yourself. You will benefit by focusing your mind and will on the things that are truly important to you.

Mission Begets Vision

As we settle on our purpose in life, we cultivate a vision – an aim that we want to achieve. For example, if you find that your purpose in life is to create happiness, then you can take that excellent aim in any number of directions. Walt Disney took that mission and created exciting theme parks, redefining our society's whole notion of amusement. You don't have to do what he did in order to fulfill that mission. You can find your own unique expression.

Suppose you enjoy performance, perhaps comedy will bring you closer to fulfillment of your quest to create happiness? How about combining your mission with a variety of talents like cooking and decorating? You could be like Martha Stewart! If you are a teacher, then this could find expression in workshops designed to show ordinary people how to live free and happy lives. Frankly, the numbers of ways we can express our purpose are close to infinite. Very few of them are "wrong," although we'll discover that not all of them are profitable or enjoyable. Just trust the process – trust that as you pursue your purpose, all these little visions will sort themselves out quite nicely.

Purpose Powers Hope

What's true for us as individuals is true for our hope. Hope is not connected to works, rather to purpose. We've all known people who have worked hard, so hard they've exhausted themselves, and yet they were still hopeless. They couldn't see a bright tomorrow no matter how hard they labored. That's because hope isn't manufactured by our effort. Hope is really a byproduct of our identity and our vision.

When we know who we are, and when we have a destination (no matter how far off and away), we have the necessary elements for hope. We have great reasons to remain buoyant, even during the hard times.

Life isn't about self-improvement - **it's about living well.**

Accept the truth and search diligently to see who you really are. Then express your true heart and soul. You'll find more than enough hope for the daily struggles, no matter what happens.

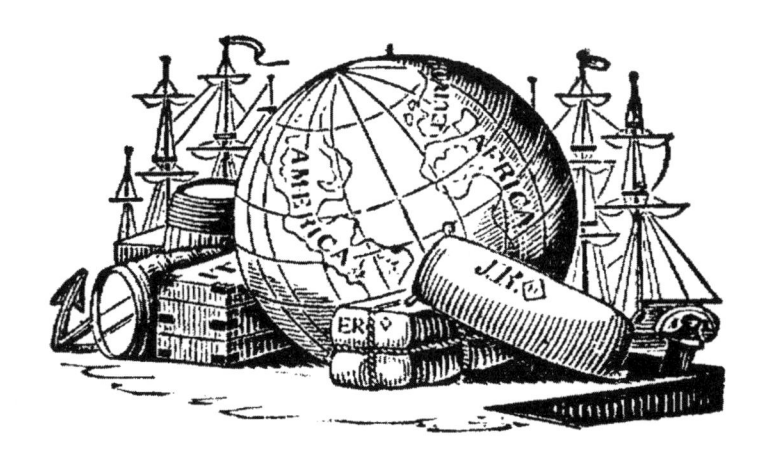

Chapter X

People of Vision

In which we learn the value of vision and discover that the vision can be written down and used for our benefit.

It was early March, and I was in Jefferson City, the capitol of Missouri. I had spent a wonderful day with an intelligent group of non-profit, nursing home administrators, and I had some time to do a little sight seeing.

As we say in Rugby, North Dakota, I had "driven the town around" six or seven times, so I parked and walked up to the capitol building. To me the grounds looked veritably lush (compared to the Dakota snows) and the weather was delightful although they said it was cold. I climbed the impressive stairs and wandered directly into the rotunda.

Looking up, I just had to stare. There on the high walls surrounding the great circle, carved in marble for all to see, was this great truth:

"Where there is no vision the people perish."

What an amazing statement! The more I thought about it, the more I realized that vision is central to life. There are few things as deadly to our soul as aimless, wasted, meaningless effort. Truly, without a vision people perish.

Friends, if the builders of the Missouri State Capitol knew the importance of a vision to the political and social process, (important enough to carve in stone) surely we have to discover its importance in our individual lives.

Hope and Vision Look Forward

Vision is a key element of hope. People of hope have a real vision: a look to the future of what they **want** to happen; a picture of what will be; a clear thought of how their purpose in life will be demonstrated.

> *...if we have no clear vision, we're like a blindfolded person who's spun round three times and tossed off a moving bus...*

Whereas a mission statement is a general expression of "who we are," the vision is a more particular focus toward what we want. Simply said, if we have no clear vision, we're like a blindfolded person who's spun round three times and tossed off a moving bus, we don't know where we are or where we're going. We only know it hurts.

If we don't know where we're going, how on earth will we ever know if we've arrived? Vision is important in every part of the journey, motivating us to start, focusing as we proceed, and clueing us in when we have achieved our aim.

A vision provides us with a destination in mind. Hey, that's the purpose for sailing in the first place. Even a pleasure cruise leaves some place, goes some place, and returns to some place.

Vision can be imparted

Having a vision may sound easy, but sometimes it is very hard. We may have been brought up with some heavy duty, negative expectations. We may think the whole world is against us, so why bother to have a vision? Or the vision we've acquired may be so bleak and sad, it wears us down just thinking how bad things are.

Sometimes we really need someone to have a vision for us. For a lot of folks, this comes in the family setting from parents and even from siblings. But if we've missed it there, we really just need a teacher or a friend to see us with hopeful eyes. We need somebody to care enough to look at us and see a "future."

I was working once with a group of Native American nurses from a reservation, and we were talking about hope and vision. Now if you know anything about reservation life, it is fraught with some mighty tough health and safety issues. For instance, here in North Dakota diabetes runs rampant in the Native American population. It contributes to terrible health problems and untimely death. There is nothing pretty about diabetes, and the folks who labor to battle it are modern heroes.

We had just talked about having hope for ourselves and for others, and I asked, "Can anyone give me an example of a problem that you face so we can think about how to tackle that with a vision?"

There was a long pause, and then an older nurse leveled me one of those awesome looks that arrest your attention and freeze your blood. "Yesterday this happened," she said. "What could I say to the 16 year old girl who said to me, 'My grandmother's a diabetic, my mom's a diabetic, and I'm going to be a diabetic. Why shouldn't I just do whatever I feel like doing and eat whatever I want, cause it won't make a difference.'"

Silence. The others shook their heads and sighed. It was a familiar story of hopelessness.

Of course, I was stunned. What on earth could you say to a young person who wants a normal, fun life and only sees the whole deck stacked against her? Would it help to just tell her "Eat right. Exercise. Take your medicine. Behave." Would it?

Yet her deep problem wasn't lifestyle, it was lack of vision. All that young lady could see was darkness and failure. What did she need instead?

Then it struck me. She needed a truthful vision – a picture of her life from somebody who could see a very different future for her than the one she saw for herself.

"What do you think would have been her response if you turned to her and said, 'I see you, a healthy grandmother, sitting out on the lawn in front of a beautiful, well kept house, with your husband at your side. All your children are gathered around you, having a cook out, while your grandchildren are playing and running around, in a safe clean, neighborhood?'"

The nurse looked surprised and said, "Wow."

Chapter 10: People of Vision

You see that's the power of vision. Without it, the people perish. They really have nothing to live for, and nothing to sacrifice for because their vision is limited to the immediate moment. They are a forgotten generation that forgets they are raising the next generation.

I believe there are many such hopeless people because they have no vision greater than themselves and no perspective longer than today. They seem to know that today sucks and tomorrow will be just like it, only more so. They are disconnected from the work of the previous generations and have no sense of destiny; they lack the knowledge that they are building "tomorrow."

How do we give them hope? In vision – in a vision greater than themselves and bigger than their current abilities, loftier than their fears and mightier than their comforts. They are just as "called" as you and I; they have a purpose for being here. Certainly they sense that sad, empty feeling of unfulfillment and are not sure if anything can be different. Without a vision the people perish for lack of hope, so we can help them best by planting seeds of vision.

A vision statement is simply a strategic intention of how you want to express your purpose in life.

Write Your Vision Down

A vision statement is simply a strategic intention of how you want to express your purpose in life. There is no set way of doing it, no magic phrase that has to be a part of the vision. It is personal, and a personal expression of YOU.

Vision statements need to be written, and I like to do this in two stages.

The first is to write a statement, like a headline, simple and direct. It reads like a conclusion. For example, there is a medical facility whose vision statement reads "To be the best, most innovative health care provider in the state."

That's a nice headline. It gives you a snapshot of what they want to accomplish and what they think is important. As far as I'm concerned, your personal vision statement can look like anything – anything that you find meaningful, that is.

A vision headline can start out with "to be", or "to have", or "to see":

> ➢ To be a teacher who really cares about kids and makes a difference in their lives.

> ➢ To have a zillion dollars.

> ➢ To see the inner city cleaned up and filled with justice.

> ➢ To be the best, most involved mother in my family's history.

> ➢ To have a heart for the lost and downtrodden.

> ➢ To see the things I invent help every person in America.

Let your sense of purpose guide your vision statement. Don't worry right now about how corny it may sound, or how incomplete. The important thing is to get the headline written.

Now Launch the Second Stage of the Vision Rocket

Far too many people and organizations stop at stage one. They have a mission statement and a vision statement headline, and they figure they've got everything they need. In reality, there is nothing magical about the vision statement. Just having one and writing it down won't guarantee that it will happen. There are no magic pills. The magic of the vision is YOU.

That's why I find it helpful to write out **a detailed picture** of what the vision is, and to use "outcome language." The second stage is to flesh out, in real observable terms, what your vision headline will look like when it arrives. Write down the outcomes

... I find it helpful to write out **a detailed picture** *of what the vision is, and to use "outcome language."*

that you'll see when you reach your quest. An outcome is a result, something concrete that you can see and touch and smell.

Let's take the vision headline "To be the best, most involved mother in my family's history." You might think that anyone could read that statement and know exactly what is meant by it. Wrong! Each of our definitions as to the meaning of "best" or "most involved" will be different, as different as our family histories. Therefore, to make this vision statement come alive with passion, we need to make it speak to us in concrete, outcome language.

(Please understand that the following example is for display purposes only. I may have been called a mother, but I am not an expert. You are free to totally disagree with the word pictures that I offer – after all, that's the whole point of making a vision statement your own.)

Start by thinking about what a good mother does, how she acts, and the way she holds herself accountable; the kinds of things she would always do and the types of things she'd never do, the monkey business she won't put up with and the family values she'd encourage. Think of how various situations will turn out and the kind of relationships she will have with her children, spouse and friends. As that picture gets clearer, you start writing it down as you see it. (Oh yes, write it in the first person, using "I" statements.)

> "I am involved in the PTA, and am happy to go to the meetings because I know that I have something valuable to contribute, even if I don't know much about what is being discussed. I know my children's teachers because we are a team. I greet them by their first names and am comfortable to call them on the phone if I need to because they know I will listen to them and work with them.
>
> "My kids and their friends are welcome in the house. Once a week I bake healthy cookies and everyone can have some. I see my children playing musical instruments and practicing each day after school before they go out and play. Every night I spend special time with each child, no matter how young or how old,

and I tuck them in and make sure that I tell them I love them.

"My husband and I agree on a few, simple house rules. Moreover, we discipline the children with the same level of reward and correction. I never shake or strike my kids, no matter what, but if it's necessary, I swat them once on the backsides with an open hand to get their attention, and then I carefully train them what to do. I don't count 'one – two – three' and then get up to deal with a problem. Even when I'm tired I rise and deal with trouble because I am consistent. And no matter how naughty a child may have been, I always make sure they know that I love them when I have to correct them."

Do you see how the language is a mix of coaching (with phrases like, "I am consistent" and "we are a team") and of outcomes (results that I will see when the vision is fulfilled)? In this example, the outcomes include being an active member of the PTA, having house rules, and standing up to deal with problems even when tired. Those are outward signs of my inward victory (i.e. being the best mother I can be).

Because I have taken the time to write this down, I have centered my undivided attention on the vision. I know this vision intimately. It means something very important to me. When I read it I get excited all over again because I am passionate about the results. My detailed vision helps me keep my hope focused. THIS is the future I want.

Of course, I can add to it, subtract, or revise the outcomes. That is only natural. As I learn more and do more, I'll come to have a deeper understanding of what I want and who I am.

You Can Catch a Vision for Others

People need hope. We need hope for ourselves and we need others to have hope. Catching your vision, for yourself and for those you love, is a powerful and genuine way to build hope.

As a parent you can write vision statements for your children. Having a vision for their success and happiness is a crucial part of raising them in a hope-full environment, but for heaven's sake, don't heap a lot of unrealistic expectations on them.

A vision statement for little Sally needs to be growing document, because she is a growing person. As **she** develops, the **vision** should develop. The closer the vision mirrors her purpose in life, the more helpful and hopeful that vision will be, and that's what you want. **The vision flows from our love for her, not to make her lovable.** As you gain an understanding of her purpose in life, you can begin to see a vision with clarity.

To say "Little Sally will be the first female President, winner of the Nobel Peace Prize by age 7, and prettiest girl in the world" is destructive, cruel, and outrageous. Those kinds of goals aren't based on **her purpose** in life. They are based on our own selfish ambition. Great parents don't do that. Great parents have a child for the sake of the child, not to satisfy their own needs. We don't want to live our lives through our kids; we want our kids to have quality lives of their own.

Visions are Simple and Practical

Good visions arise out of simple thoughts. For instance, I'm sure you want Little Sally to be happy. Therefore, think of the answers to this question: what does a happy child do?

A happy infant is held a lot, talked to, played with. Therefore a good vision for a little baby would include those kinds of outcomes.

A happy grade schooler is held a lot, listened to, given the opportunity to make some decisions and voice opinions, able to participate in grown up activities like setting the table, washing the dishes, and making cookies. A good vision statement for the grade schooler will include those kinds of outcomes.

As Little Sally becomes a teen, her purpose in life will have many more opportunities for self-expression. A good vision for a happy teen would include outcomes like participating in selected sports, group activities, late night honest conversations, and permission to apply wide-ranging decision-making.

You'll know the right things to envision as you think clearly about what it means for each particular child to be happy, productive, involved, educated, and kind. A vision that consists of those anticipations will surely build strong children of hope.

Vision and Hope Look Forward

Why does vision work? What are my reasons for making the time to create vision statements for myself, or with my family, or for an organization?

Think of life as a race. In every foot race there is a finish line that must be crossed. You can't win the race without crossing that line.

In fact, you can't even get credit for participating in the race unless you cross that line.

Let's be practical. No one runs a race looking backwards. You can't even run a decent race if you are busy looking sideways at the other racers next to you. In order to do your best in a race you **keep your eyes on the finish line**.

In the race of daily living, your vision (your statement about what you want) is the finish line. All through the day you look ahead because you want to cross that line in the best time possible. That is why vision contributes to hope, because you aren't intimidated by the things that have been or by the bustle of the crowd around you. Your focus is on the end point and every day is a new race.

Vision looks up and ahead, not back and aside. Therefore, aim your focus through the circumstances, across your situation, toward the solution or goal you want.

Hope Anticipates

When we look up and ahead, we are anticipating. Anticipation is based on a future hope. I like to make a distinction between "expectations" and "anticipation." There have been times when I've been really upset and disappointed because my expectations weren't met.

Expectations are dangerous things. We create them based on past performance. Therefore we expect tomorrow to look pretty much like today.

If expectations were only applied to our own behavior they wouldn't be quite so bad. But you know what we do? We place expectations on others. Even though we don't control them and don't have a right to command how they will think and act, we build emotional, unrealistic calculations, which will always let us down. By playing the expectation game, we create little self-fulfilling prophecies as to how people will act or respond.

Expectations of Others Leads to Disappointment

Often, we guard ourselves by expecting the worst; we expect that our brother, who has always been mean to us, will be mean to us again. We may think, "Perhaps he'll be nice this time. Then my negative expectations will be exceeded and I can be happy, and if he's mean – like always – I won't be so disappointed." Expecting the worst doesn't really help us because we invest inordinate amounts of emotion and mental energy, and are regularly disillusioned.

Then again, to make matters worse, we tend to set unrealistic expectations of others. This is particularly true when we get emotional around the times of the high holidays like Yom Kippur, Thanksgiving, or Christmas. We just take a wild shot as to how everyone else will behave and how they'll act when they see us. Of course, since the expectations are unrealistic

Expectations are dangerous, but anticipation is fruitful.

and unfounded, they never come through as we wanted. No one rushes out the door with wild abandon, sweeping us into their arms and weeping for joy. Instead we walk into the house, unassisted, and somebody nods at us and says, "Oh, you're here." This leaves us angrily staring at our emotional ruins, thinking to ourselves, "See, I should have expected the worst. Things will never work out. No one will ever care about me." Meanwhile, your loving family is wondering why you are always so sultry and mean-spirited at family events. Maybe they should have expected the worst of you since you have obviously rejected *them.*

What a muddle.

Expectations are dangerous, but anticipation is fruitful. When I anticipate, I am focused on my own vision and on how **I'll feel** when I cross the line. I am not holding others captive to my expectations; I am holding on to my own passion and concern for the happy outcome I am aiming at. If I expect anything, it is the expectation that I will fulfill my own purpose this day, and cease looking to the others to fill my void.

As I look to the future with hope, I look with anticipation. It's like that ketchup commercial when they play Carly Simon's song, "Anticipation". We wait eagerly for that wonderful, unpredictable moment when we get what we want.

Can your Vision be Wrong?

Many people are quite confused by vision – how will they come up with one? How will they know they have the right one? What if they're wrong? They are focused on the legal aspect of having a vision, and it isn't any fun for them. It's just one more requirement that they have failed to meet.

... the most important thing is this: if you want a vision, **get one**.

Let me comfort you. Vision isn't a law, it's just a useful tool that will build your hope and help you to fulfill your destiny. No one from the vision police will try to arrest you. Vision isn't work; it's simply direction. A good vision flows out of your purpose and aims at things you really want to see accomplished. Your vision helps you pilot the sailboat; because you have picked your direction you can intelligently use your boom and rudder, (i.e. your choice making and change making).

That is why the most important thing is this: if you want a vision, **get one**.

It's that simple. Pick what you will, and go for it. The important thing is to have a vision and be about it. Right or wrong is meaningless until we get in motion. Without some kind of progress in any direction, we have no need for correction. Who cares if something is right or wrong if we simply aren't going to do it anyway?

Momentum is in your Favor

When you're in the middle of the ocean and every direction looks exactly like the other (just as good and just as bad), then you have to pick one and go for it. You can't steer a ship that's dropped anchor. **Only a ship in motion can be directed**, and only a ship at sea can use the winds and waves to its advantage. Trust in the fact that as you go along, your vision will be refined.

Steer after something good, something you have some passion about. If you find it helpful, think about some piece of society that is rotten to the core, some injustice that drives you nuts, and decide to dive in and heal it. Alternatively, think about the activities you most enjoy and how you could fill 18 hours a day with them. Pick something good, not just for yourself but something that is good for others too, and then start moving toward it.

Your passion and your purpose will surely be exposed.

Someone had to be the first to build hospitals, or to create social service programs. Somebody had to build the Seven Wonders of the World, and somebody had to be the first to write about them or to travel to see them. Somebody had to be the first to fight against slavery or to fight for the rights of women. What could you be the first at?

"But Bob, I don't have the money. I don't have the time. I don't have the smarts. I don't have the team to back me up."

GOOD. Neither did they. You are in the perfect position for a vision - all heart and much lack.

William Jennings Bryan, the old American Statesman, said it very well:

> ***"Destiny is not a matter of chance,***
> ***it is a matter of choice.***
> ***It is not a thing to be waited for,***
> ***but something to be achieved."***

Life isn't about self-improvement - **it's about living well**.

Catch a vision and go for it. You will discover that life is more satisfying because you are moving forward in destiny. People of hope know the value of anticipation, and however long it takes to cross the vision-line, they are in the race for good.

Chapter XI

Measure for Success

In which we come to see the value of feedback. Knowing our results is absolutely essential to producing good outcomes.

Have you ever looked at the old maps from the early seafaring days? The coast lines of Europe and most of the African continent are remarkably detailed and exact. But as you look to the West, there is nothing but ocean, and at the edge of the oceans are drawings of sea serpents, kraken, and dragons.

Centuries may have passed, but people are still people, and when we don't have good information we tend to "fill in the blanks." When we don't know something we seem to insist on supplying answers. In the face of the unknown we let our fears fill in the missing pieces. Those map makers could have drawn angels, or the lost continent of Atlantis, or a setting sun. Instead they populated the vast oceans with perilous monsters.

With so much global travel and information, it's hard for us to feature the fears that an explorer like Christopher Columbus had to overcome. Granted, he had a great theory, that the earth is round and therefore the ocean we look at on the East must be the same ocean the Asian's look at on the West. Yet when he consulted his maps, where did they tell him he was heading? Straight into the mouth of a dragon!

Christopher Columbus must have been a good hope-er because he knew the journey was worth the risk of facing the unknown. He must have had that deep seated sense of destiny that he was on to something great. Despite other's warnings and the tales of fearsome sea creatures, he greeted the unknown with anticipation rather than fear, and his hope sustained him, as well as the many sailors who traveled with him.

Christopher Columbus had to overcome.... when he consulted his maps, where did they tell him he was heading? Straight into the mouth of a dragon!

When you're sitting at the dinner table across from Queen Isabella, it's easy to talk about the bold adventure you intend to take. But in the middle of the ocean, with nary a smidge of land in sight, what keeps a Columbus going? How do we keep the ships together and keep our hopes up as we sail "off the map" into uncharted waters?

Christopher Columbus knew a great truth: you have to measure your progress to feed your hope.

Success Requires Measurement

We need to measure how well we are doing because hope is fed by forward progress. There is no substitute for accurate information. Whenever we try to achieve something, we need to know how well we are doing. That is called feedback. Without feedback it is impossible to get any sense of achievement or progress. Even if we are not weighing hope directly, by measuring a few well-chosen outcomes we fuel and preserve our hope.

True North

As a youth (lo these many years ago), I was with an intrepid group of campers, canoeing through the beautiful Boundary Waters between Canada and Northern Minnesota. About three days out, our leader dropped our one and only compass into the middle of a lake. He was more than frustrated; he was scared. He tried for over an hour to find that thing to no avail. He was so upset he made us all pull over to the closest shore while he got out and paced at the water's edge.

Never one to keep my mouth shut, I took him to task for having such a snit. "It's just a little compass. Forget it. We've got maps."

He stared at me like I'd just fallen in from an alien planet. "This isn't downtown Minneapolis. You can't just look at a map and know when to turn right. There are no city blocks; no street signs. You have to know True North to navigate!"

Let Your Vision be your Star

In the middle of the Atlantic Ocean (let alone the middle of Basswood Lake), you have to get your bearings; you need to know True North so that you can judge where you are now, how well you're progressing, and what you want to take for a direction tomorrow.

Sailors have many tools, like sextants and compasses that they use. In the still of the dark night, under a clear sky, they look up into the heavens to find Polaris, the North Star; the one star that never seems to move from its place in the cosmos. When they know True North, they have concrete information to identify their position and to plot their future course.

Even landlubbers need a star. What do we look at to see how well we are doing? We look to our purpose, and most particularly, to our vision.

Your vision statement is an elegant summary of the future you want. Within its details you have already established a set of outcomes (results) that you desire. Now you need feedback that relates to those specific items.

What you know makes a Difference

Whatever it is that you want is what you must measure. In management circles they say that you must inspect what you expect, otherwise you won't get respect. In other words, people will try to do whatever you demonstrate that you care about.

Inspecting the outcomes at work is the best way to show you care. It doesn't matter what brilliant thing you say in a team meeting, or how good your intentions are. Until you get off your chair and go look to see what is happening, people won't care about it any more than they perceive you do.

Chapter 11: Measure for Success

Having written your vision in detail, you have made your targets plain and clear. Every time you pick up that piece of paper you are reading your word picture of the future. Most people never make the time to do that, and they suffer for it. Even more people never make a plan to measure their progress. They are like sailors who never navigate their paths through the ever-changing seas. We cannot trust to our instincts alone that we are heading in the right direction; we need concrete, objective information.

When you really want to make a difference, you have to survey your effectiveness. Pick a few things to measure – some outcomes that are part of your vision. By inspecting them (i.e. measuring your progress) you will naturally raise your own respect for those outcomes. You will have proven to yourself that you really care, and your determination will respond to the challenge.

> *When you really want to make a difference, you have to survey your effectiveness.*

Quality Measures for Quality Results

If this sounds like a Quality Assurance process to you, it is. You are assuring to yourself that you are aiming correctly for the quality life that you want.

I stand in amazement at the way people resist taking measurements. I know we don't always like accountability or the judgments that come with missed targets, but I wonder, is it possible something else is afoot? Could it be we know how powerful measurement is so we are afraid to unleash it? Or is it that every time we try to measure things it is a dry, thankless enterprise, instead of fun?

Feedback can be Fun and Rewarding

When people get feedback, they naturally alter their behaviors to get more pleasing results. Peter F. Drucker, the management expert, says that feedback is one of three things necessary to create responsible workers. The other two elements are meaningful work and continuous learning. Let's apply that model to our own life.

To be a responsible hope-er we need to be **doing something meaningful**. Since the ultimate target of our living is to fulfill our purpose in life, I would argue that there is nothing as important and meaningful as that. It is meaningful not only to society at large, but it is personally meaningful. That's a one-two combination of significance.

The second element is continuous learning. Drucker makes a distinction between training and learning. Training is the learning of work tasks and procedures. **Continuous learning** however is a deeper process. For instance, rather than only being trained where to put the rivets on the wing of a plane, continuous learning addresses the underlying issues:

- how a plane that is heavier than air flies,
- the physics of stress that dictate why the wings are designed the way they are.
- concepts in aerodynamics,
- how the team works together
- the reasons for these particular production standards.

Continuous learning is never finished. There is always something more to know, something more that will develop our understanding and insight. The more we learn the more depth we bring to our experiences.

Finally, responsible hope-ers get feedback. **Feedback**, the third element, is simply information that relates to whatever it is that you are doing. A basketball player needs feedback about making baskets. If he is blindfolded and deafened, how will be ever know that he has made points? Because he gets feedback, he changes the way he plays the game. He learns how best to make shots from various parts of the court. Often, because of all the continuous practice and on-going feedback, he knows he's shot a basket just by the sound of it.

Feedback Informs Your Hope

So what does feedback look like to a normal person who has some hope? It involves measuring/checking/looking at results. It compares the vision outcomes to the reality of production.

Let's say your purpose in life is to help people; you want to make a profound difference in the world. Since helping others is what rewards you, measure that. Articulate the outcomes you want to see (and be as exacting as you can). Set up simple checkpoints where you'll look to see how well you are meeting those standards. Because you have the outcomes written down, and because you are willing to check them regularly, you are more than likely to accomplish them. You will naturally, even subconsciously, work to achieve your ends.

Measuring what happens is an important part of the process of keeping your hope real. Sometimes we humans are a slippery bunch.

We may think we are right on the beam, only to discover later that we traded in our outcomes for a few tasks. I call this phenomenon "Task Shift," when we measure tasks instead of accomplishments. In a hospital this would be likened to a surgeon who cut someone open and sewed them up again, but didn't pay any attention to whether the patient got better. "I did what I was supposed to. I completed my tasks. Doesn't that count?" To be honest, it doesn't count at all.

It's Results that Count

Successful work is all about getting results. A company that can't get results (such as to make 100 widgets and deliver them by Friday) is a company that will go out of business. Who wants to buy a bottle of shampoo that is empty, or go to a fast food restaurant that is slow, or attend a dance without music?

Customers demand something for their money. It would be a sorry Post Office if all they could assure you was that someone would walk by your house, yet refuse to promise that your mail will be delivered. It isn't the tasks that count; it's getting the letters to the right people that matters.

The same is true for us as individuals. When it comes to our purpose in life, we don't want to simply take a stab at it; we want to actually do it. The results we get, or don't get, are meaningful to us. When we get information about our outcomes, we know something important.

We naturally modify our behavior based on our results. If the outcomes aren't pleasing, then we'll make changes to try and get greater success.

You Can Change Tomorrow

Tomorrow always gets built. Tomorrow comes whether we are prepared or not. What should matter is that tomorrow looks brighter and sharper than today. The influence we wield is intended to express our calling and our identity.

Unless we actually do something, tomorrow will come and we will have lost the opportunity to shape it. Or rather, we could say that we have helped to shape it by refusing to do anything **today** that would have made it different.

When you are surrounded by water on all sides, with only a few monsters on the edge of the map to keep you company, your measurements will help you endure. Your hope will be strong because you will be gaining good, objective information about where you've been and where you are. Your sense of progress holds you to your purpose, even if you haven't made all the distance you had wanted to. The fact that you have taken in valuable feedback helps you anticipate a better tomorrow.

> *Tomorrow always gets built. Tomorrow comes whether we are prepared or not.*

When we get the feedback we need, related to our purpose and our vision, we help ourselves put our best hopes to work.

Life isn't about self-improvement - **it's about living well.**

When we actually care about what we do and the way we do it, we'll care enough to check regularly to see that we are making a difference.

It's worth the effort, because feedback knowledge gives us intelligent information we need to make changes. Its the results that count. So let your hope have full sway and measure your influence.

Chapter XII

Dream – Believe – Plan – Do

In which we learn the orderly progression of how to turn our dreams into living realities.

Some years back I was working with a group in a nursing home setting. Their mission was to create satisfaction by delivering excellent nursing care to those in need. However there was a problem. They had an increasing number of Alzheimer's residents who were having real trouble in the normal nursing environment.

Alzheimer's disease attacks the brain, and it does more than just wreck one's memory. It slowly and cruelly destroys one's personality as well as the ability to perform normal living functions like dressing and shaving. Because Alzheimer's is a disease of the brain, outside stimulation that you and I take for granted and ignore (such as music playing in the background or noisy machines) is like running fingers down a blackboard to Alzheimer's victims. They can't make sense out of their environment, it over-stimulates them and they often act out with negative behaviors. So these poor folks are confused, feeling lost and forgotten; the whole world is irritating and baffling to them. They need a quiet, well-ordered, calm environment that will allow them to do the things they still can while assisting them with the things they can't.

Due to the design of the building, and to the lack of money, it was impossible to build some fancy new Alzheimer's unit and move them out of the regular nursing setting. At first glance it looked like an unsolvable problem. Too bad, so sad, you're had.

However, hope is catchy, and when there is a person of hope around, somebody else just might find the courage to try something different. A bunch of us met as a group, talking about the problem, expressing our desire that something should change for the better, and confessing our disappointment that we couldn't do the ordinary solutions.

Someone finally threw their hands up. "What good are we doing? We can never afford to build new beds and we can't reconstruct the beds we have."

That's when somebody piped up, "The problem isn't with beds. Our residents don't have trouble when they're sleeping. The problem is when they're awake. We don't need beds. We need to create a special space and run a program just for them during the day, every day."

The room was eerily quiet for a moment, and then suddenly everybody was talking at the same time. "It could work!" "We could use that one activity room that nobody uses." "We need to go to other facilities and see what programs they are doing so we

CHAPTER 12: DREAM – BELIEVE – PLAN – DO

can learn from them." "My department will repaint, wallpaper, move walls, whatever you need." "I'm going to call that professor at the university, she had great ideas."

In a heartbeat, everything changed because our vision changed. Instead of trying to do what others were doing, somebody looked at the honest need and came up with a great solution. (I'm happy to report that the Alzheimer's program even won a special state award as a 'Best Practice.')

It's what you Can do---not what you Can't

Vision is powerful when it's linked to what will happen when we DO something. Focusing on what we WON"T do or what we DON'T do, will never get our rear in gear to actually GO DO.

A whole lot of politicians talk about what they don't want: they don't want war, they don't want pollution, they don't want people in poverty. Well, I don't want those things either, but talking about what I don't want will never move me to action. We generate action by insisting on what we **do want**. I want peace. I want clean air. I want everybody to have a good job. Those are vision statements that have the potential to move us forward. You just can't beat a good positive statement for kinetic energy.

The time has come to think about what we CAN DO, and get our eyes off the CAN'T.

The Action Process

There is a little formula that I think describes the process of how to move ideas into action, and turn action into success. I have seen this operate many times in corporate work settings, and I'm convinced it works equally well for us as individuals.

I call it **Dream – Believe – Plan – Do.**

This orderly progression is logical and easily applied. Each step simply follows the one before it, laying the groundwork for the one to follow. It is useful when you are setting goals or mapping out solutions to your current problems. In either case, you can use this when you want to organize, motivate, and install fresh changes.

These changes can be little or vast, it really doesn't matter. On some level all change is resisted, so it is important to keep your shoulder to the wheel and press the process into motion, because the reason for all the work is to get new, improved results.

It Begins with a Dream

A **dream** is the starting place for all positive changes. These dreams are little pictures of what we'd love to see. A dream is like a vision, only not as precise. It usually is generic, but it tends to be quite emotional and passionate.

Lots of people have lots of dreams, and for most humans, it all stops there. They never seem to engage the dream and take it to the next level. That's because it costs you nothing to dream. Dreams are free, and are cheaper by the dozen.

Dreamers and schemers don't make it. In North Dakota there's only one rule to remember when you drive the country roads: stay between the ditches.

Dreamers, who won't do anything except dream, are caught in the one ditch of paralysis. They have wonderful thoughts and brilliant aspirations, but the rest of their life is in neutral with the parking brake engaged. They don't even want to work on the dream. They'd rather just meditate on its virtues. Better yet, they can hardly wait to get the next dream. Their dreams come and go, and stay as dreams.

On the other hand, schemers, those folks who are constantly manipulating and hatching plans, are caught in the other ditch. They aren't paralyzed – they are in constant motion and want to get everyone else into motion, only they have an over-arching goal of self gratification, thus they are engrossed with nonstop, useless activity. They don't want to go anywhere in particular; they just want the world to be whirling. They may be busy (and they are perfectly happy to make you busier than they are), but they really have no goal in mind or purpose at hand other than the selfish pleasure of keeping everything and everyone in motion.

But oh my, if you have a dream that you really want to come to pass, a dream that you want to be more than a day dream, you have to **believe** in it. People are created to be believers. Believing is something everybody can do, regardless of education, social standing, or physical power.

The Second Point: Believe in it

Believing is incredibly powerful and central to our character as people. If it took mountain climbing to be a success, there'd be many of us who'd never have a ghost of a chance. If success required that we sustain an emotion (any emotion) for 48 straight hours, most of us couldn't do it. At some point we'd lose emotional intensity. If our success meant that we had to pass some IQ test at 120 or better, then most of us would be disqualified; we just wouldn't be smart enough. It's a good thing success simply requires belief.

That's the amazing thing about believing – anybody can do it. You can be emotional as a volcano or as inexpressive as a pancake, yet believe in something. You can be intellectually as sharp as an isosceles triangle, or a blithering idiot, and it won't affect what you believe, or your ability to believe. You can be strong as Hercules or a complete 97-pound weakling – either way, you can believe and be motivated by those beliefs.

We Do What We Believe

One of the things that psychologists know about us human beings is that we act consistently with our beliefs. If I believe that I am a screw-up and will always fail, then I act that way. If I believe in a moral code, I will generally behave according to that code. If I believe my Mom and Dad love me, I relax when I am around them because I know I'm safe.

That's why it is so important to know and to believe the truth. Whatever we believe will guide the things we do. If we believe really bad things, even lies, then we will act in accord with those lies. It is part of the job of this book to help you challenge your beliefs, and to pick up positive beliefs so that you can be a successful person of hope. Believe me, beliefs are central to your behavior.

How do we Believe in the Dream?

You begin by believing that it is important to do. The first step in moving your dream into reality is to become convinced that your dream is a good one.

Once you know inside that the dream is outstanding, then the next step is quite logical: you need to come to the belief that **you and your team** are the ones to do it.

When you believe the dream is significant and that it needs YOU to do it, then you will naturally believe that the dream is worth the cost of making changes, spending some money, and re-tooling your life. In short order, you will discover that you believe the world will be a better place by making this dream a living reality. Likewise, you know that it will be poorer if you don't.

The power of belief comes from the fact that you have counted the cost. You KNOW that it's worth your sacrifice, and you KNOW that humanity can't thrive without it. From this conviction springs the personal power to push on through the resistance you are sure to encounter.

Because we believe the dream, the likelihood that we will actually carry out the plans that we make is multiplied. Surely we've all gone through those goal setting exercises where we write out goals and then write out objectives to accomplish those goals; and yet, when we return to "real life" we never, ever implement a single feature we planned.

There are two basic reasons this happens:
1. The goals aren't related to our real, personal dreams, or
2. We haven't come to the place where we believe the dreams are worth the effort.

You can FEEL that a dream is swell, but until you come to the place of conviction about it, it will stay a dream. Since we do the things we believe, when we believe in our dreams we are naturally predisposed to make our beliefs come alive.

Make a Plan

Once we have a dream and believe that dream, then (and only then) are we ready to **plan**.

Planning is important because it doesn't leave your dreaming up to chance. A plan is a thoughtful, written approach guiding your action.

Good plans address the things you need (like more education, training, equipment, and helpers) as well as the things you want (like witty inventions, the use of your resources, and the steps you'll take to make things work).

Good plans start with the present realities and move to the future, step by step. Once you have a plan, you can make assignments to take action.

With the Plan in Hand — Go Do It!

Which leads us to the final piece of the pie: **Do**. A plan isn't worth the paper it's written on if nobody will do it. In my experience, this is the most exciting and challenging stage of the process, because this is the time when your dream will be really tested. Especially if it costs money.

Don't wait till all the money you need comes in. It will never arrive and your plans will lie dormant. I have always found that when you are pursuing something good with good motives, the money will be there when you need it.

Don't wait until you know everything that needs to be known, because you will never be smart enough to know everything. I have always found when you are sincerely pursuing something, you are open to learning and will acquire much more "know how" than you can get ahead of time.

Don't wait till everybody else thinks your ideas are great, because they won't. I have always found that people resist new ideas, even good ones. The only time when people appreciate your dream is once it is established, functioning and successful. If everybody you talk to likes your dream, it probably means that it has already been done.

"The Truth will out."

If your dream is good, if you believe it, and if you have made reasonable plans, then by taking action you will succeed. Good dreams seem to come along at the right times, and the money, support and guidance that you need will be there, if you don't lose heart and **keep on doing**.

> *Don't wait till everybody else thinks your ideas are great, because they won't.*

It costs nothing but brains and time to go through the first three points. As valuable as they are, they have taken a minimum investment. What makes them important isn't their cost – rather it is their power to motivate and guide our activity. When we have a plan that leads us to the outcome we believe in, we have all it takes to maintain our hope, even in the face of great obstacles.

People of hope are people with a vision. Not all dreams become visions, but each vision starts as a simple dream
– a dream powered by purpose.

Life isn't about self-improvement - **it's about living well.**

Quality living is full of hope, and hope is full of vision.

Dream – Believe – Plan – Do is the way you can take a vision and bring it to action.

Chapter XIII

What Will You?

In which we discover the power of the human will. The will is greater than our emotions and intellect – it is the part of us that makes choices.

We are not in control of what life dishes out to us. We are only in control of how we react and respond to life, and where we decide to go. Our **will**, working with our desires, is the part of our character that leads us into quality living. Not our emotions. Not our intellect. Not our physical needs. It is our will. Thus the real issue for quality living is in our will.

Humans are Choosers

The amazing thing about us as people is that we are choice-makers. We are designed to choose what we will do. It is part of what makes us uniquely human. I cannot think of any other created being that makes choices like we do.

Animals are motivated and must respond to the basic forces that act upon them. Their emotions, their thoughts, and their physical bodies command them. In essence, they have an urge, and they do whatever they must to satisfy it. Like us, they can learn to respond to stimuli in various ways – in fact, they can learn to be helpless – but humans possess a power of will that makes choices beyond the drive of instinct or the reward and punishment of behaviorism. We are even able to make informed choices to our detriment; even knowing that the consequences will hurt us, we may well go ahead and make that choice.

A lion that hungers must eat. He doesn't care what he eats, antelope or water buffalo; if it is edible he will dine. A lion may starve to death, but not because he has failed to exercise a choice. He will starve because he is too sick to hunt, or because all the game is gone.

When a lion is angry, he doesn't think about it like we do, he simply smacks whoever has annoyed him with a paw. An alpha male, when threatened, will always physically attack to assert its authority and status. It cannot exercise discretion about who it will attack or when. When provoked, it will attack, acting out its instinct and emotion. When a lion is fearful, he must flee or fight. He does not make a choice about it, he responds to the drive.

When a lioness moves into a heightened chemical state, such as the estrus cycle, she must mate. A male lion will fight to mate with her, even to the death. His body drives him. He doesn't make a choice, he responds to stimuli with direct, programmed action.

We are Different for a Reason

People are different. We are designed to choose. Our emotions, our intellect, and our physical urges are subject to our uncanny ability to make choices.

When we are hungry, we can choose **not** to eat. We can deliberately go on a 40 day fast from food in order to accomplish something that is important to us physically or spiritually. Even though food, shelter and security are our most primal needs, we can elect to go without in order to accomplish a greater goal than the satisfaction of those needs. Mother Teresa and Gandhi are prime examples of this type of sacrifice.

When we get angry, we can choose to forgive, or we can choose to get revenge, but it will be in a time and method of our own selection. We can relish the emotion of anger or hate it; the anger does not have to control our lives. We make a choice about it. We will not act until we have engaged our will.

When we are afraid, we choose whether to fly away, fight, or to simply take a stand because we are convinced that what we are doing is right. As powerful as fear is, we have all had the experience of being very frightened, while still going ahead and working contrary to that fear. It may have been in the third grade, stepping out on the stage of the elementary school to recite a poem, or it may have been standing up to that bully who made each day a personal hell of fear. For some, it came as an act of defiance to the control of parents or other authorities. In any event, we each have learned that we can feel the fear yet still act out a choice despite our alarm.

When our bodies send out strong chemical messages, we always have the power and the right to choose how we will act on them, or whether we will take action at all. There is no mandatory mating season for males and females. Our bodies have to wait our good pleasure to act. Some people even make the conscious choice to never mate; they live a celibate lifestyle because they have determined a greater good is accomplished than if they were to satisfy their urges. By like token, no one makes you marry. A male and a female make a mutual decision that transcends their physical drives, intellects, and emotions. They choose to love one another and choose to do something about it, publicly and legally.

Our "chooser" is very powerful; it takes precedence over our feelings and our brains.

Making choices is a great part of what life is all about. Our "chooser" is very powerful; it takes precedence over our feelings and our brains. We can make some really stupid and damaging choices in a heartbeat, or we can forego a choice, biding our time for years. All of our action depends upon our "chooser" – no choice, no motion.

Ships at Sea

Like a ship at sea, to keep moving the sail must be able to use the power of the wind. "Luffing" is what sails do when the wind and the sail are not in optimal position to each other. The sail luffs, like a flag, along the same line as the wind. When a sail luffs, you know that it is not using all the available energy.

Good sailors watch their sails and when they see them luffing along the edges, they reposition the boom which pulls the sail tighter against the wind. This causes the boat to remain at peak motion.

Your will is your sail. When you make a determination and raise it up on the mast of your desire, you still need to position your will relative to your environment. Like a boom, the choices you make either pull your will up tight against the situations and circumstances, providing you with forward motion, or your will luffs and you lose momentum.

If a boat comes to a dead stop in the water because of careless piloting, the only way to recapture the wind is to get up from your seat by the rudder and push on the boom with all your strength to force the sail into position. Until that boom has been forcibly manhandled into a working position, you can't go anywhere.

Our Will is Revealed in our Choices
We know an awful lot about emotions and about thinking processes, but there haven't been many studies as to how the will works, or if there are "types" of will that are common to people. What we do know reliably is that we have a will, and that all the other elements of our personality are secondary to our will. We can use our will to help ourselves, or to destroy ourselves. Once the choices are made, we act them out and no emotion or thought or physical danger will turn us from the path. The will is awesome and powerful. When used for good, it is a beautiful well of life. When used for evil, it is as terrible as an atomic weapon.

So what controls this awesome mechanism of choice? It is our belief structures. What we believe inevitably finds expression through what we do, because we make choices based on those beliefs, and we do not take action until we have made a choice.

We Always have a Choice
I've talked with folks who tell me that I am wrong. They believe there are certain reactions that are far beyond their control. Typically, they tell me that certain strong emotions demand instant action, without thought or application of the will. It isn't a choice with them. When they get angry they **have** to hurt someone. They are justified in this behavior because "They made me angry. I didn't have a choice."

Could they have done something differently?

Certainly. Otherwise every effort to negotiate peace between nations and couples would fail 100% of the time. It is inevitable that someone will make us angry. What is not guaranteed is how we will respond to the anger we feel. We are even free to forgive.

If you believe that every time you have a strong emotion like anger or fear, you have to strike back to get even, then you will choose to do that. Even though it may feel like an automatic response, you are actually making an informed choice based on what you "know" to be true. You just "know" that you are justified when angry because "that's how the world works."

Strong and Weak Responses

Our will is shaped in the same fashion that our emotional and intellectual makeup is constructed – one judgment at a time. What we conclude about our experiences is what shapes our beliefs. That is why two sisters can grow up in the same environment and yet have very distinct interpretations and beliefs arising out of their shared experience.

Each sister may have heard the same message from her mother: "Why can't you be as pretty and as good as Little Lulu next door? What's wrong with you?" To one, this provokes a belief that she is broken, ugly, unable to measure up; she is defeated before she even starts the race.

The other sister just knows that her mother is wrong and that her life will be different because she is going to be popular, active, and productive. Her mother's cruel words act like a challenge she will overcome, rather than a conclusion, overcoming her.

There is nothing better than having strong, loving parents in a secure family relationship to provide the foundation upon which you build your life. However, did any of us have perfect families? Yet, even in the worst circumstances, we are not hopelessly lost. We can always change what we choose to do. Our beliefs are not set in stone, and applying truth will modify them.

Our Judgments Create our Interpretation

When we embrace the truth, we almost always discover that we have wrongly interpreted some aspect of our history. We have leveled a judgment that was off the beam, and our life has suffered for that. To correct the damage we have to declare the truth and wrestle with it, applying it consciously, and choosing to act in accord with what we now know is true.

That is why I am convinced that what really shapes us isn't the experiences we live through; it is our **judgments** about those experiences. Therefore, we can change at any time. We do not have to wait until we have a bunch of good experiences before we can enjoy a quality life. Rather, we can reassess our judgments and our beliefs, and apply truth in the face of our current situation. By changing our "insides" we ultimately change our "outsides."

When we embrace the truth, we almost always discover that we have wrongly interpreted some aspect of our history.

If you are not pleased with your behavior, then you have to look at what you really believe. You may say with your mouth that peace is a good thing, but if you really believe that the only way to have peace is to make everybody else do things your way, then you will make choices consistent with your high estimation of yourself.

Moreover, I can guarantee that people won't like you very much or appreciate your judgments about them and their free choices.

The Staying Power of the Will

The human will is very powerful. Once the decision is made, the will is in full action, and it can maintain that activity until it is satisfied. We've all seen it, people who have "made up their mind" to do something, and they keep trying and trying until they succeed.

Some like to think that they are not "willful," that they don't have a will of their own. This is patently false. Every person has a will and every person uses his or her will. It's just a matter of how they use their will that seems to make it look like they aren't making decisions.

One can subjugate their will to that of another, but even in doing that, they are exercising a choice. It may not be a good choice, but they have chosen it nevertheless.

The will is like a light switch. It is either on or off. There is no half way. When a choice is made, the switch has been turned on. Till then, it is off waiting for connection.

Kathy Kolbe, in her book *The Conative Connection*, asserts that there are three parts to everyone's personality. Psychologists call these:

> **Cognition**
> **Emotion**
> **Volition.**

Cognition is your ability to think. It is the part of you that reasons and analyzes.

Emotion is your ability to experience feelings. It is the part of you that feels.

Volition is your ability to will – to decide to do something. It is the part of you that initiates action.

She uses a wonderful example to show that the will is something separate from the other pieces of our personality. We've all had a similar experience, lying in bed half-awake, chilled to the bone because all the covers are down around our ankles. We lay there still as stone, even though our reasoning mind is awake enough to do some thinking. It says, "You are cold. There are covers down there. If you wake up you can get them. Of course, if you wake up you won't be sleeping anymore and you are tired. What a dilemma."

Your emotions are working too. You feel uncomfortable. You wish someone would do something to make it all go away. You are upset that you have to lie there and be miserable. Even so, these emotions do not move us.

If you want to know what your will feels like, it is the part of you that suddenly snaps into action when you rear up in bed, grab all the covers you can get, and flop back down for a few minutes more of sleep. Until your will is engaged, you'll lie there forever uncomfortably.

The Will Takes and Maintains Action

When the "order of the day" is to get something done, you need your will. By setting your will on an object or direction, you are actually commanding all the other parts of you to get in line and to follow through. That's the way it is meant to be.

Your will is like a gear. It must be in motion and engaged to make a difference. If the will is engaged but not in motion, everything is frozen in one spot. Likewise, if the will is merrily whirling around but not meshing with other gears, its power is lost. Only when the will is engaged and in motion do changes occur.

Now, there are some whose emotions seem to lead them through life. They are convinced that emotions are compelling and motivational. "If I can just get the right feelings, then I will spring into action."

Certainly I agree that emotions are motivating, but they are not sustaining. Emotions poop out. Even negative emotions like depression and anger lose their steam over time. We don't need our emotions in order to do things. We only need to make choices to generate action. Once we are in motion, we discover that our emotions follow along. That's the right order.

Then there are others who are highly intellectual. They just know that brainpower is everything. They rationalize their behavior and constantly seek after knowledge. "If I learn enough and am smart enough, I'll be right enough to be motivated to action."

Certainly I agree that the intellect plays an important role in every human endeavor, but it is not our smarts that motivate and sustain us. The mind and all its glorious reasoning is meant to supplement the will. We make choices based on our beliefs. Ideally our beliefs are informed by our reasoning mind, but that is not a requirement for action. Once we have initiated action, then our brains work to support the very task that we have set our sights to accomplish. Minds left to themselves are prone to wander and daydream. The mind is a terrible thing to waste – and thought that is disconnected from action is a waste indeed.

Like a sail, our will is designed to be lifted up and positioned in order to make full use of our environment. Purpose and intellect and emotion will all play their part in helping us make our choices, but when no choice is made, our will is misused and all the power of our direction and circumstances are lost. One simple goal, common to all sailing is this: keep your sail up and full of breeze.

Our Will Motivates our Hope

When we look closely at the soul of the average human being, it is clear that the main job of motivation and diligence belongs to the will. The emotions and the intellect make their contributions, but when it comes to simply getting up and doing something, that is the will's job. Sometimes it isn't any fun.

That's why emotions and intellect let us down. They wear out under pressure. However our will can be set like stone, and nothing that comes against it will turn it from its course. Because the will is connected to our beliefs, it is essential to our purpose and our vision. If the purpose is great enough, we will choose to hold the course until we get what we want, or die trying.

Jenkins' Law: Everything is Tested!

When I was a kid, every first Wednesday of the month, they would test the emergency alert system, and blow the air raid sirens. Every television and radio station would regularly hold tests. You'd be doing your homework, listening to something, and suddenly there'd be this piercing whine, followed by an announcement, "This is a test of the Emergency Broadcast System. This is only a test. If this had been a real emergency, you would have been directed to run around in circles, screaming in desperate panic. Since this is only a test, you can stare blankly at the wall and in five seconds we will return you to your normal mind-numbing broadcast."

Have you noticed this great "law" at work in the world - that every idea, every action, and every person is tested? This is a universal law; it applies to everyone in every culture in every age.

Everything is tested.

No one is exempt from the test. It's like the law of gravity. You can believe it or disbelieve it; still gravity holds you close to mother earth. You don't have to take my word for it. Just walk off a cliff and you'll discover that the law of gravity is still happily at work. In the same way, you don't have to take my word about testing – it won't change a thing. You'll still be tested. Bad people and bad ideas are tested, and just as surely, good people and good ideas are tested.

> *This is a universal law; it applies to everyone in every culture in every age... Everything is tested.*

I think there is a reasonable explanation for this: only those people who pass the test are allowed to influence the world. Whether for good or for ill, one must pass the test in order to proceed.

As we said earlier, dreams are free. What keeps all these millions of dreams from happening? Very simply, people will not push on to the next level to make them a reality. When the testing comes, it is easier to let go than it is to push ahead. Alternatively, when people DO push through, they are believers in the dream, with a plan, who want more than anything else in the world to make it a living reality. They are what we call "do or die" people.

So what will you?

Life isn't about self-improvement - **it's about living well.**

Hope is a matter of will. Applying our will is the secret to achieving smooth sailing through the many circumstances we face day by day. It is also the secret to achieving the purpose for which we exist.

Although our emotions and our brains are important, it is our will that separates the victorious from the defeated. Quality living is full of the anticipation of victory, therefore it is full of choices that are taken rather than ignored.

Chapter XIV

Flames of Desire

In which we examine the role that desire plays. Desire, like the mast of a sailing ship, holds the sails open to catch the wind. Our will, like a boom, pivots on the point of our desire.

So far, I've mostly described how your "chooser" works in a passive way that relates to your experiences, responding to stimuli whether it's internal or external. The most remarkable feature about your will is that your personal power to choose is the greatest force on earth to initiate action.

The Will is Designed to Initiate Action

Your will is designed to originate creative energy. You can make something new or restore something lost, redesigning the world according to a fresh plan. This right belongs to every person on earth in each generation. This right to create and recreate needs only to be initiated.

Yes, it will be tested, because the law of testing is universal and unavoidable. That is why your action must come as an act of the will. It takes your will to make something out of nothing, sailing against the currents and tides. Without determination, there is no influence.

That is why the closest companion to our will is our desire. When we want something, we are likely to choose actions that will achieve those wants. When we want to reach a goal, or to solve a problem, then our will, working with those special desires, turns us into people who take action without first waiting for a reaction.

Desire = Want

It is as true as truth itself: you've "gotta wanna" or you won't act. You've "gotta wanna" or you'll take a few preliminary stabs at something and then give up. You will face the test and lose. You've "gotta wanna" or you can't use your will no matter how rational, logical, good and pleasing you think a course of action will be. If you don't want to do it, you won't.

Too many of us are convinced that our desires are somehow corrupted. If we desire something, we immediately think of the hundred reasons why we **shouldn't** want it. Obviously, not all desires are equal, and not all the things we desire are good. I'll be the first to tell you that I don't want evil people to get their evil desires satisfied. I am very happy to see them frustrated when they'd like to go kill somebody, or rape, or pillage.

But we have desires that are inherently good. The desire to share our love. The desire to establish justice. The desire to be recognized and to give recognition to others is really a good thing. If we shut down all our desires then we are losing the good along with the bad. Our ability to hope is compromised by such a decision.

Designer Desire

We are designed to desire. When we **want** something, we get connected to it. When we want something it is personal. When we don't want something, we are distant, aloof, and uncaring. When we are forced to do something, unless we find a way to want to do it, we are begrudging slaves, forcing ourselves to take each step, constantly searching for creative ways to get out of the work. That is why we are great workers when we are willing, able, and desirous, and why we are so pathetic when we lack those elements.

We need to care. What we care about, we care about. What we want, we want. My wife has a rule of thumb in our house – we have to care. When a child or a visitor is asked, "Would you like regular milk or chocolate milk?" The answer, "I don't care," is NOT acceptable. When she hears that she looks them straight in the eye and says, "No. You have to care. So tell me what you want." Often it leaves kids dumbfounded (not to mention adults). But she is right; we all have desires and preferences, let's express them honestly.

> *My wife has a rule of thumb in our house – we have to care.*

It seems so simple that one shouldn't even have to address it; however, I am constantly amazed at how we lose sight of the simple motivating forces in our life. How often we set our wants and cares aside. Sometimes we can feel quite noble denying ourselves, (and sometimes such a sacrifice is noble), but most often we use this as a smoke screen. We are afraid of our wants, afraid of what they reveal about us, and afraid that we can't satisfy them. This fear is what turns hope into an academic exercise instead of a living reality.

I am not advocating that we become the most selfish people on earth. There are plenty of more important things in this world than what Bob Jenkins wants at any given date and time. However, I know that I am motivated by some very deep and wonderful desires – desires that go beyond my mere comforts. These desires are so intense I sometimes can't even sleep. I lay there thinking about how much I want to accomplish them.

Our Purpose Births Many of our Desires

Sadly we shortchange ourselves by only allowing the desire of things that don't count for much (like material goods and comforts) while ignoring the things that really do matter (like justice, or fellowship, or mercy).

We are human beings. Let's be real, we are made to want. It's hardwired right into us. Whatever it is that we want, we want. Some things we want so deeply we can hardly stand it. What might we accomplish, how deep would our hope go, if we really gave ourselves over to our keenest desires?

We each have a special, unique purpose, a core reason for being here on earth - right here, right now - yet we let it lay dormant, unconnected to our wants and desires. We may feel that little "tug" on our sleeve, reminding us that we'd like to care, but we are callused and ignore it. Go figure!

A Quality Life is Connected to Quality Desires

To have a quality life, we need to be quality people, connected to our purpose, full of hope, sailing through every hour of every day toward the targets that move us strongly. We are most fulfilled when we are connected to the deep things that move us, when we are people who care.

Chapter 14: Flames of Desire

That's risky, isn't it? Some of us have learned that if we want to safeguard our emotions, the thing we have to do is to NOT CARE. When we don't care, nothing bothers us because we have no stake in life; however, when we **do care** we can be hurt.

When we care, it makes us feel bad to miss our targets. When we care, deeply and truly, we are vulnerable – open and visible, liable to be criticized for the things we believe and do. Yet, when we really care, (and I mean REALLY CARE), then we just can't help taking the risk, because the thought of winning through to our target is far greater than the price we have to pay today.

Therefore, care about it. Be intense about your desires, about who you are and the purpose that propels you. That alone, almost more than anything else, will carry you through the lean and difficult times. Intensity is a delightful and necessary component to achieving your purpose. Let's be frank, why would you want to spend your life pursuing a purpose you really don't care about? Therefore, care deeply and intensely.

Recently I encountered the Hugh O'Brian Youth Leadership organization (nicknamed HOBY), which does leadership training with sophomores in high school. Sitting in an auditorium with about 300 other parents for our orientation, we were taught among other things to stand up and cheer out loud.

If you want to feel foolish when sitting with a group of strangers, that's a great way to do it. Obviously, most of us were pretty wimpy when it came to hollering the cheers. I suppose that is why the first cheer that they taught us was about enthusiasm.

Here is how I "cheer" it around the house.

> "To have enthusiasm you must be enthusiastic.
> To have enthusiasm you must be enthusiastic.
> To have enthusiasm you must be enthusiastic.
> Boy, am I enthusiastic!"

The Blessing of Enthusiasm

If you ask me, this is the right order. If we wait for enthusiasm to catch up to us, we are like the people who wait until they can afford to have children ... they never have them. Children are priceless, and therefore they are fabulously costly to birth and raise. We'll never be smart enough, rich enough, or safe enough to have kids. The best way to have them is to want them, and then let all the rest sort itself out. Whatever we need to learn and however we need to change, can all be done once we've begun the long, important journey into parenting.

We live in a cynical age that belittles enthusiasm, and there are many, unfriendly jokes about enthusiastic people.

Similarly, if we wait for an infilling of enthusiasm **before** we will be enthusiastic, we will never be enthusiastic. Acting enthusiastically is how we generate enthusiasm.

We live in a cynical age that belittles enthusiasm, and there are many, unfriendly jokes about enthusiastic people. The sad fact is we are afraid to be enthusiastic. We certainly don't want to stick out of the crowd, or be the butt of some joke. Like the parents at the HOBY meeting, we sit around trying not to be abnormal. So we linger and wait until the whole group is enthusiastic, and then maybe, just maybe, we'll join in with them. What a waste.

Life is Full of Resistance

To excel with intensity, we have to sail against the current of the times. This was ever so. To have a hope that makes a difference, we have to act out in hope. To fulfill our purpose in this world, we need to be about it. We have to be hopeful to have hope!

There is no replacement for caring. If you find that it is hard for you to care - if too much of your daily life is spent trying not to care, then it's high time you applied the HOBY principle to your situation. To really CARE you must first do some CARING. Don't wait until your emotions are at a fever pitch to dare to take the risk. Begin now by simply caring about someone and something. Build care by caring.

Declare that you Care

The concept of desire is closely related to declaration. We initiate action by making a declaration, even if that declaration seems to fly in the face of the facts that surround us. Reasonably, it only makes sense. If everything were perfect, what would we have to do? Therefore, in any journey toward something new, we are going against the trend of the day. We haven't arrived, so we can only declare that we are going to make a difference, and then live that way. We have to act enthusiastically to generate enthusiasm. In the same way we have to make a declaration of truth in order to generate truthful living.

When our desire and our will is activated, we are in the perfect position to catch the wind of our environment and start toward the object of our heart. Now we are a soul ablaze with the passion of motivation. We are initiating our movement, not just waiting to react to the next thing that may happen. Like the captain of a ship, we are choosing a direction and doing the things that are necessary to get there.

Let Your Desire take Fire

Hope is inclusive – involving the whole person. Although hope isn't dependent on our brains, our feelings, or our bodies, it works to enhance those aspects of our character. When we are people of hope, we are activating our whole person into quality living.

Take account of what you pay attention to. You may have great desires, and make great declarations about what you intend to accomplish, but if in the midst of that you turn your focus from your hopes to the rocks beneath the waves, or the uncertain status of sea and sky, you will surely fail through fear.

People become what they focus on.

People become what they focus on. When you focus on your self, you become selfish. Focus on others you become other-ish. Turning your focus to a caring direction makes you a good servant. You are able to keep your own integrity while at the same time you look out for others.

Strategic Desire

I have clearly seen this principle in business settings. Take for instance the typical work of a focus group. A focus group gathers customers together and directly asks them pointed questions: "What are we doing well? What needs to be improved? What do you like? What puts you off? What do you need? How do you want it? Can we serve you better?"

Chapter 14: Flames of Desire

The goal of a focus group is obvious: focus on the customer. Get real facts and make changes as a company to fulfill the corporate mission by better serving your clients. By focusing on others, a company can become what it needs to be to fulfill its purpose.

I have also seen this principle used negatively. Take for instance the common morale committee. A couple of managers and a handful of employees focus intently on the emotional state of the company's workers. By turning the focus away from quality production and aiming it toward how bad the morale is, the more the company becomes exactly like what it is looking at. The attitude and the emotions of the employees (especially the verbal negative ones) become the focus. Invariably the purpose of the company and its customers get lost in the process.

Always focus on the things that matter: your customers, your service, your dreams, and the team's solutions. Since we become what we focus on, choose your point of focus wisely.

When corporations, just like individuals, focus on the good things that are bigger than their own needs and wants, the better able they are to "live their mission."

Therefore, focus on your desired outcomes; how it will look when the vision comes to pass. Then you will be filled with vision. Focus on outcomes and you will be inspired with solutions to the problems that seem so large. Focus on others and you will naturally reach beyond your self-absorbed limitations. That's a wonderful way to put your desires into action and to translate your vision into reality.

Hope is Real

Hope isn't idle wishing – it is connected to the ideal, to the desire and beliefs you hold dear. Let the flames of desire burn, and use their light to inform your hope. Set your will to achieve your purpose – desire that above all else, and you will focus on that with a vigor that will surprise you.

Although I am only an amateur historian, I find many concrete examples about what is required to achieve a quality life in history. Take for instance the importance of Valley Forge.

The Three Critical Choices

Once the colonies on the East Coast of the Americas declared their independence, they had to fight to make it happen. Nothing ever comes easily, and this was certainly true for them politically, economically, and socially.

The British sent a large contingent of their best military forces, under some of the wisest generals of the day, as well as throwing in a few thousand mercenaries hired from Prussia. King George was not going to simply lay down and play dead. The colonies were to come back into submission willingly, or be forced into it. He offered no other options.

The Revolutionary War was a long tiresome affair, characterized by many more defeats than victories for the Americans. Although we had a brilliant military leader in George Washington, and despite the intensity of our clever politicians, the country wasn't unified in its conclusion that the war with Britain was worth it. Plenty of citizens actively resisted revolution, and a greater number sat off on the sidelines, quietly hoping things would work out without requiring them to do anything drastic.

Chapter 14: Flames of Desire

The name Valley Forge doesn't mean much to people today. They might remember that it had something to do with the War of Independence, but beyond that they are clueless.

Valley Forge was the winter camp of the Continental Army. After having lost a series of key battles (with one notable exception), the army retreated to this part of Pennsylvania in 1777, desiring to regroup, refresh, and re-tool their forces, only to find themselves in the throes of the worst winter they could remember. The weather wasn't the only problem; there weren't enough blankets or shoes, let alone food stores and munitions. Medicine was at a premium, and most who got sick just went without. Disease ravaged the ranks of the army. No matter how hard Washington pled for assistance, there was little. Morale was understandably low, and every hope and dream that the army stood for was challenged beyond belief.

There were only three things that one could do at Valley Forge. The first was to **die**. Many did. Best estimates are that 3000 soldiers died there (and another 1000 were too sick to fight or move) – that is a 33% casualty rate!

They weren't bad men; they were working for a noble cause, doing what they believed was best, and yet the test required their supreme sacrifice. It only seemed to make matters worse that they were dying in winter camp rather than in some valiant, pitched battle against the redcoats. I'm sure they wondered, "Have I given my all in vain?"

The second response was to **desert**. Many did. About two out of every ten men simply packed up and disappeared. All they could see was despair, destruction, disease, and disaster. Who would want to stick around for more of that? Even the shame of being a quitter wasn't enough to deter them. Fear has always been the great enemy of hope, and these good men were sore afraid.

If you didn't die and you wouldn't desert, only one other response remained: **desire**. Those who stayed rose up from the test with a determination and desire for victory unequalled in those perilous times. No one could have predicted what passion and patience those survivors had, because they didn't just hang on by their fingernails, they determined to thrive in their adversity. They rose up with incredible commitment - they would win or die trying. There was no other option.

King George, backed by all the wealth and power of his established nation, could not deter them any longer. They were ready to win for they had passed the test - and friends, win they did.

Valley Forge choices are still the choices that we have to make. Rarely are they as big and dramatic as the actual event, but we still have three responses to the challenges of life. We can die. We can desert. We can desire.

The choice is ours. No one else can make it for us. It's a matter of our own will.

Choose to Hope

It is hard to know what is the best decision sometimes, because if we don't have a heart for the outcome, then perhaps it is the best thing to bail out and let someone else try and tackle the situation. Sometimes things are truly beyond our ability to choose. It's a sobering thought that there are no guarantees. You can be a good person, doing a good thing, and still die. Having a heart full of hope doesn't change that.

The key issue is simply to have hope no matter what. If one is going to die (and we all will some time) then would we prefer to die in a hopeless state of despair, or in a buoyant state of confidence? It may not seem like a great choice, yet this is key for quality living. **Hope is always worth it.**

Life isn't about self-improvement - **it's about living well.**

In all circumstances, it is our ability to choose that makes us potent agents of change. Yet life is full of testing like the seas are full of wave and whatever you desire to pursue will be challenged. Passing the test is the only way to make dreams come true. It takes uncommon desire married to your will to create a future – a future that reflects your purpose. Hope is found in the hoping. Hope fuels your will and your desire, because it stands above the circumstances. The situations of life do not define you, you move in the hope and anticipation that **you will define them.** That's a hope that counts for something. That's a hope that overcomes.

> *It takes uncommon desire married to your will to create a future – a future that reflects your purpose. Hope is found in the hoping.*

Chapter XV

Optimism: The Language of Hope

> In which we examine the role of optimism. What we think and what we say have direct influence on our ability to endure. Hope helps us to endure the testing, because we know we are pursuing our purpose.

I'm sure you've heard the familiar description that the optimist thinks this is the best world ever, and the pessimist fears that he's right. Nevertheless, there is a greater difference between optimists and pessimists than seeing the donut versus only seeing the hole: optimism is a key component of quality living.

As research on optimism and pessimism has been mounting over the last three decades, we have learned that optimists tend to have better health and recover from health crises faster. Optimism constructively feeds your immune system, while pessimism wears it down. Optimists will rise up to do better after a defeat whereas the pessimist will surrender or perform at a lower standard. Optimists tend to be higher achievers; even when life gets them down they don't stay down. Pessimists are far more prone to depression — terrible depressions that last longer than two weeks at a time.

> *...we are not born optimists or pessimists; we have **learned** to be one or the other. Whatever we have learned, we can "unlearn" and "relearn".*

Endurance — persistence — perseverance — these are character traits that follow optimism. This is natural since they arise out of a belief that today's victory or defeat is not forever and always. "Try and try again" is the song of the optimist, while the pessimist lacks the conviction to rise to the occasion.

We can Change for the Better

In his seminal book, *Learned Optimism,* Dr. Martin Seligman explores what he believes are the root causes of pessimism, depression, and optimism. He makes a compelling case that we are not born optimists or pessimists; we have **learned** to be one or the other. Whatever we have learned, we can "unlearn" and "relearn".

A pessimist isn't a bad person. Pessimists are people who have bad, personal explanations for all the things that go wrong in their life — explanations that convince them that there is little reason for hope, and no reason for taking action. Likewise, an optimist is someone who explains the negative things quite differently. When Dr. Seligman and others studied this phenomenon, they saw that optimism and pessimism run along two dimensions of belief: permanence and pervasiveness.

How you Explain the Outcomes of Your Life Determines Your View

If you believe the bad things that happen to you create a permanent negative situation and that they ruin almost everything in your life, then you are telling yourself a pessimistic explanation. For example, you are unexpectedly told that your position at work is eliminated due to the economy and the company's fiscal policies. Let's assume you liked your job, so this is bad news to you.

If you're a pessimist, you would greet this information by reeling into depression. The more you thought about it in your head, and talked it over with your friends, the more you would explain it as a permanent and pervasive problem. "This kind of thing always happens to me. If I weren't so stupid I'd have gotten out long ago. I was going to go out of town this weekend, but this wrecks everything. Why bother to try anything at all, it just always goes wrong."

If you're an optimist, you would feel just as bad as the pessimist does when bad things happen. The difference is that the optimist has a different explanation for what has happened. The optimist sees the bad as a temporary, not a permanent problem. Instead of it being pervasive, ruining everything in ones life, the optimist sees it as being limited. Using the same example, let's listen in to the optimist's explanations. "I feel so bad because I really liked that job, but at least I can get another. If management wasn't so stupid they would be doing better in the marketplace. It's a good thing I'm going out of town this weekend, so I can have a good time and forget about this for a while. Then on Monday, I can put some things in motion."

What's interesting is that when it comes to the good things that happen, the pessimist and the optimist change places. Optimists explain the good things that happen as being permanent and pervasive – things are great now and will be for a good long time; this one good thing just makes everything else even better. Pessimists have their good days too, but when they happen they explain them away as being temporary and limited. They expect "the other shoe to drop" tomorrow and they know that the happy event is solitary.

> *Optimists explain the good things that happen as being permanent and pervasive ...*

Change How You Talk

Essentially, what we say makes all the difference. Our explanations, to our self in our brain or with our mouth to others, affect our optimism. One of the impressive tools for bolstering hope is to get a handle on what we say.

By deliberately speaking hopeful truth out loud, we can change what we believe. This means that when you need to get a grip on your pessimism, you can acknowledge the truth that the bad things are only temporary and limited, and use your mouth to express that new belief.

Control What You Can

It is amazingly difficult to change how we feel or how we think by focusing on what we **won't** think or feel. It's rather like the old dilemma, "Don't think about pink elephants," and then all you can think about is pink elephants. Or when you are quitting smoking, if you constantly dwell on "I'm **not** going to smoke - I'm **not** going to smoke," you'll have spent your whole day thinking about smoking. This is NOT HELPFUL when your goal is to stay away from cigarettes.

However, when it comes to our mouth, we have control. The things we speak out loud, even to ourselves, carry a weight of conviction with them.

When our mouth says, "I'm going to have a good day today," our brains and our emotions rally and go to work to make that a reality. Similarly, if we say, "I'm going to have a horrible day today because my kids are mad at me," then our soul goes to work to agree with that expectation.

The mouth has tremendous power to bless or to curse. (Just watch me when I do plumbing for a practical demonstration.) With our lips we can praise someone, reward them, direct them, respect them, honor them, and help them, or we can run them down, punish them, defy them, belittle them, dishonor them, and deny them.

The Mind is Great at Remembering

I'm sure you've heard the analogy that compares our mind to a tape recorder. As we go through each day, we play various tapes in our mind. Some are helpful tapes of encouragement and direction, while other tapes focus on our failures, our inadequacies, and our hopelessness. There are moments when it seems we can almost hear those familiar thoughts in the voice of our parents, siblings, or friends.

It's no wonder. How do we think those thoughts got in there in the first place? Because someone spoke them to us and we drew our own conclusions about them. We heard something and made judgments.

Perhaps your mother said casually one day while fixing your hair "Your hair is so thin and useless. No one can do a thing with it." She was expressing her irritation over her own inability to help you, but what did you hear? Perhaps you concluded, "She's right. My hair is bad. I am bad. My hair will never look good. It's hopeless to try." Perhaps you got angry; "I'll never be a bad mother like her, running her children down. I hate her for hating me." It's our interpretations, not our memories that create the problem.

These little tapes verify our beliefs. "I'll never get it right." "I'm a screw-up." "Of course I'm not loveable." "It will never change. Everything is ruined." These belief statements stem from our earlier judgments.

However, **they are not permanent.** They can be changed. Just like audio tapes, you can choose which ones to play and which ones to leave on the shelf. When you want to gain self-control over your thoughts and feelings on the unconscious level, consciously use your mouth.

Rewriting the Tapes

You start by picking up the truth, and asserting your will. Example: you are downsized. The truth is that you are not a bad person even though you lost your job. Your whole life isn't wrecked despite the fact that you need employment. You may be inconvenienced, even offended, but you can create solutions to the current problem.

When you hear yourself using permanent and pervasive explanations, you'll have to argue with yourself. That's what an optimist does. Optimists argue vehemently (strongly and vigorously) for the truth, because they know the present reality isn't final, tomorrow is another day, and they are free to change.

Whatever we have learned, we can learn again, and learn better. That's the power of hope. Use your mouth to make a positive difference in your own behalf.

Positive Speech Begets Positive Feelings

Dr. J. Mitchell Perry, in his book *The Road to Optimism*, makes a strong case for using what we **say** to influence what we **do**. He talks specifically about the "language of exclusion" and the "language of inclusion."

When we speak in the language of exclusion, we are talking about what **ISN'T**. Likewise, when we speak in the language of inclusion, we are talking about what **IS**.

The classic case of this is to approach a normal American family leaving the amusement park. Assuming that they had an average happy experience, what would you expect the children to say to you when you ask, "How was it?"

> *When we speak in the language of exclusion, we are talking about what **ISN'T**. Likewise, when we speak in the language of inclusion, we are talking about what **IS**.*

"Awesome. Cool. I almost puked on the roller coaster of death. It was great!"

Ask the parents the same question, and they say,

"It wasn't bad."

Whoa! What just happened there? If something is "not bad" does that mean it was good, or can it mean just about anything?

Talking About What Is

Children naturally speak in the language of inclusion. They talk freely about what they see, think, and feel. When they share their feelings they do so with honesty, (ask any parent who dragged their kid along to Aunt Mabel's house for a boring visit). They talk freely about their opinions. When they speak it is done with the definite inclusive assurance of a natural born optimist.

Guarding Ourselves with our Language

Somewhere in the process of becoming adults, we learn to hedge our bets and to hide our true selves. We learn to talk in exclusion. We freely offer our assessment of what ISN'T, rather than go out on a limb and take a stand for what IS.

Let's say you have a great idea at work. You can hardly wait to get to the boss the next morning, because you know this idea is going to change the world. You stand there by the boss's desk, breathlessly awaiting her response, when she looks up with a little shrug; "I don't have a problem with it."

What does that really mean? First of all, it is hardly a ringing endorsement. Second, it clearly shows what she was thinking the whole time she studied your idea, "What's wrong with this thing?"

Chapter 15: Optimism: The Language of Hope

We even do it with our friends and family. "Why don't we go out to eat?" Stop and think what you're really asking for – a list of reasons why you should stay home and eat peanut butter and jelly sandwiches. The language of exclusion is more than just negative; it fuels bad thinking and bad relationships.

Dr. Perry's assertion is that if we change the way we speak we will change our inner sense of optimism, and we will create an optimistic environment around us. People will see us as positive, assertive, truthful, and affirming. Therefore, they will choose to hang around us, and choose to do business with us.

This positive state of affairs is reached just by altering one's language to talk about **what IS**. That kind of optimism isn't pretending or phony. It addresses fundamentally how we use our mouth to express ourselves honestly, and how our mouth sustains our hope.

Is Optimism Denial?

Optimists know that present circumstances are real – they don't deny them. They just deny the finality of them. Today's circumstances do not predict our future, nor do they lessen the worthiness of the vision we are pursuing.

The language of inclusion, besides being positive and cheery, is naturally outcome oriented. That means it is centered on our intention, rather than in some mysterious gray world where people have to read between the lines (including us).

> ...**how we talk** *about our vision and our purpose will have direct consequence on our ability and hope to one day live it.*

Hope and vision are intimately connected. Therefore, **how we talk** about our vision and our purpose will have direct consequence on our ability and hope to one day live it.

Read your Vision Statement Out Loud
It helps us to hear with our ears the things we think in our brains. That's one more reason why it is helpful to read your vision statement out loud. By talking about what you will have, in detail, you are using your mouth to activate your whole being to go to work and make it happen.

Rather than talking about your future in the language of exclusion ("I won't be stupid." "I won't be broke." "I shouldn't try to move up the ladder at work too quickly…"), you use the language of inclusion to make positive, meaningful statements, ("I will learn this." "I'll have the money I need to send my kids to college." "I will enjoy promotions at work, even if they look a little scary to me now.").

Exclusive Speech is a poor Motivator
Politicians are big on the language of exclusion. They almost entirely try to motivate by instilling fear by describing the negative consequences of **inaction**.

> "If we don't clean up the neighborhood, we won't have a safe place to walk."

> "If we don't balance the budget we won't have a strong national economy."

> "If we can't get more voters registered we won't get good representation."

Chapter 15: Optimism: The Language of Hope

These statements aren't motivating because they are spoken in the language of exclusion. Therefore, they don't draw us in. They don't provide a compelling picture of what we **will** have. They lack natural optimism.

Clear Air. Healthy Kids. Safe Seniors. Great Schools. 100% voter turn out. These are great issues and make great goals for our society.

Because inclusive language is VISION CENTERED, it is the best way to address the important social issues. Just for practice, talk about any of these issues using inclusive language and you'll discover a natural desire within you to rise to the challenge. So will the people around you, the ones you want to make your allies in your effort to enrich the world and enjoy your life.

Life isn't about self-improvement - **it's about living well.**

What we say influences our hope more than our thinking and feeling, because we can leverage our language to our advantage. Speaking about what IS rather than talking about what IS NOT, is a powerful tool for maintaining hope and sustaining your vision. A quality life is supported by quality speech. What you say is your best vehicle for self-expression and self-leadership.

Chapter XVI

PRACTICAL ADVICE

> In which we learn that advice – even when unsolicited – is best when it is practical. There are simple things that you can do to improve and maintain the hope in your life.

Now is an excellent time for some practical, earthy advice. (At this point, my children usually heave a sigh, roll their eyes, and slump back in their chairs. So assume the position and let's talk.) It's not that I haven't already offered you practical solutions; it's just that sometimes you've got to crack your knuckles, and put your hands on something tangible. Here are a few tips that make a difference.

1. When you just can't get a hopeful feeling, when everything looks bleak and rotten, when you'd rather bite the head off a serpent than do one more thing – GO TO BED.

I know I've told you that our bodies do not create hope, but when we are bone tired and altogether out of steam, we don't have the energy to embrace our hope, no matter how much we may want to. If you are suddenly depressed, or find that your hope is somehow slipping away from you, go to bed. Tomorrow is another day, and you just need to hit the hay.

2. When all you can see is more drudgery, more work, more effort, and less success, you can help yourself by measuring your progress in "clumps." When we scan the far horizon, our target often feels desperately far away. We help ourselves gain an honest perspective of forward motion by looking at the little "clumps" of progress. This is especially true if our target is very great and very distant. If we only look at the thousand miles left to go without appreciating the last hundred miles we have advanced, we will grow weary. We will feel like our hope is needlessly deferred.

It's like sailing into the wind; you have to tack to get ahead. Tacking against the wind means that we rarely if ever get to aim straight at our target. Instead we move forward by 45-degree angles, working our way ahead by turning side to side. We are doing the right thing, but our overall progress may not seem impressive. In order to reassure your hope, measure your progress as you go along, appreciating how each little "clump" has actually gotten you closer to your target. As long as you are getting nearer your destination, you are doing well.

7 Components for your Perception of the Quality of Life

There are basically seven activities that contribute to your inner sense of quality living. Psychologists know that if you have some portion of these seven activities sprinkled throughout each day, you will feel good and function with a high degree of self-esteem.

Rest

1. One of these primary activities is rest. Rest is more than just getting the sleep you need. It also includes the kind of pastimes that you find restful, like sitting and staring for a half an hour, or watching a moderate amount of television, or even reading the newspaper while enjoying the morning cup of coffee.

Different people use different activities for rest. What makes them restful is a matter of personal interpretation. My practical advice is to take a quick look at the things you do for relaxation, and then be sure to include a moderate amount of them in each day. Your handle on hope will appreciate it.

Case in point: if you relax by watching television after your noon meal, then limit it to a reasonable amount of time. Do enough of it to feel rested, but not so much that you waste your time and miss the mark. Half an hour is generally plenty, but the length of time I leave to you and your conscience. There are only 24 hours in a day. We each get the same amount, to use or to lose. Interestingly enough, you can cram a whole lot of work into a half hour, but a half hour of rest is invariably just a half hour of rest. There is no way to jam-pack extra rest into leisure or refreshment into sleeping. If you need eight hours of sleep, you have to get eight hours of sleep.

Physical Activity

2. Our bodies are made for action. They need the rest and sleep that we can give them, and they need to "get up and go." If you have a sedentary job (like I do) sitting at the keyboard for hours, or if you are a mattress tester for a bedding company, then you need to exercise every day. When we take the 20 to 30 minutes to work our bodies, it makes us feel better because it makes us healthier. Exercise need not be traditional weight lifting; it can be as simple as walking or jogging through the neighborhood, or as technical as hiring a personal trainer. To possess a sense of health we need to take what we have and put it to work.

Likewise, take a multi-vitamin/mineral complex every day. You don't have to overdo it with "mega" this and that, but giving your body what it needs to perform at full function only makes sense.

Association

3. A quality life includes quality relationships. We certainly have many needs, but we also have a powerful desire to love – to give of ourselves to others. (It sounds sappy, but it's true.) When we spend time every day together with others, we build relationships that feed our need for community and also allow us to meet someone else's needs. If you aren't married and you are living far from home, perhaps you keenly feel the loss of relationships. There is no time like the present to make new ones. Even the Girl Scouts sing about making new friends while

keeping the old, because one is silver and the other gold. Often our social solutions are closer to us than we think.

I like managing by walking around, because it not only gets me closer to whatever's going on, it allows me to spend time with people. At the same time I get some exercise by walking about. (It's a two-fer: two solutions in one!)

Autonomy

4. Americans value their independence, and starting at a very young age, we learn to define our personality by asserting it in various situations. Autonomy - the ability to make decisions about what we are going to do and think and believe - feeds our sense of liberty. Taking the time every day to exercise our choice making is important, even when our choices are not earth shattering.

In eldercare, you learn a lot about the value of independence, because you see first hand those people who have lost their ability to function autonomously. Actually, anyone in an institutional setting has lost some measure of liberty: you eat when food is served, you rise when you are told, you dress in the clothes someone else picks out for you. It is so important to feed our sense of liberty by deliberately making choices.

When we lose our independence, we lose a vital part of what it means to be human and fully alive. So order something new off the menu, drive to work a different way, go somewhere you've never been, and read something new. Assert yourself in the small things, and you will be strong enough to stand as a great person of hope. If you are a parent or someone in authority, be sure to give others opportunities to express themselves, to be real and independent.

Autonomy is important in the work place. Even if the choices are about break times or the order of work, being able to make those choices allows workers the right to be independent – to be real. There is no substitute for liberty. Since it is necessary, try your best to provide it.

Achievement

5. Have you ever had the experience of taking a long weekend or a vacation, and even though you enjoyed the R & R, you were strangely dissatisfied for most of it? Lying on the couch, luxuriating in all your freedom, somehow inside you grew irritable, grouchy, and unhappy. Your body was sending you a message: accomplish something.

We need to achieve something every day, or we lack the sense of completeness. Without accomplishment we are aimlessly wandering in circles. Achievement doesn't have to be something great. It is as simple as finishing a set of tasks for the day, learning something, putting in your eight hours of work, or meeting an objective. Achievement is as vital to our inner health as having relationships, expressing our independence, and physical exercise.

In American society this is a particularly thorny problem when folks retire. First of all, we define ourselves by what we do for a living; if we aren't doing something, then we lose our identity and feel defective. Secondly, when we detach ourselves from accomplishment we choke off an essential component to quality living. We think better and feel better when we achieve something. Starting and finishing something every day is the easiest way to maintain and celebrate our need to achieve.

Dishes in the sink? Wash them. Dirty floors? Scrub them. Unmade beds? Make them. Letters to write, e-mails to send, bills due, phone calls to make? Smile to yourself and do them. It may feel like a lot of work at first glance, but even these little activities feed our sense of achievement. Don't cheat yourself. Attain something and be glad of it.

Fun!

6. Lest you think that I am only full of unhappy, work-related advice, try this next one: **have some fun everyday!** Fun is whatever you like. If it's been about a hundred years since you can remember having fun, you are long overdue. What's really great about fun is that it usually combines many of the components of quality living: achievement, relationship, leisure and rest, exercise, and autonomy. Why do you think we like fun so well? It's because it is so fulfilling.

Have fun at least once a day. Go out of your way to do something you like. Laugh each day – a lot! Putter about in the garden, write your book, call a friend and go out for coffee, play a round of golf, beat the tar out of your buds in a competitive night of poker ... whatever. Hope may be serious business – it is certainly important enough – but there is plenty of time for the sober, tough things. Just make sure you keep a slice of good old-fashioned delight. That's the dessert that makes the meal worthwhile.

Spirituality

7. Through it all, you need the sense of peace. Do something spiritual every day. Say your prayers, meditate, talk with your Maker, read something positive, attend a Bible study, and care enough about someone else that you want their welfare as much as you want your own. These are simple activities that express your spirit.

Whole people enjoy a whole lot of hope. Rise up each day and make it a point to employ these practical, common sense activities throughout your day.

Life isn't about self-improvement - **it's about living well**.

To keep your hope vital and alive, it helps to address the quality of life components. People of Hope are people who enjoy full lives, lives that allow them self-expression and self esteem. As my Dad used to say, "One hand washes the other." Hope and life are mutually edifying. The one helps build up the other. As long as we're going to have hope, let's have it practically and abundantly. Who needs another head trip? Keep it simple, keep it fun, and above all, keep it.

Chapter XVII

The Three A's For Victory

In which we discuss the interaction of a healthy appetite, a positive attitude and a superior altitude with hope.

Why is it that whenever you teach a principle you can count on being personally tested in it? I used to think that teachers were above the students and the subject. Long ago I learned that good teachers must live the very things they are teaching or else they lack the authority to speak. It has been my goal for many years now to be someone who actually does what he tells others to do.

I had just finished a session with a small group talking about attitude, and how we need to have good attitudes even in the face of bad situations. I told my wife that afternoon that I was ready for the test. I had every angle figured out. Tomorrow I was going to be a paragon of virtuous attitude. Let a child challenge me with some kind of smart aleck response, it wouldn't side track me. Let a check bounce or a car blow a gasket, I would handle it. Let the rain pour or the mosquitoes bite, I was going to pass the test.

Unfortunately, I wasn't ready for what really happened. Right from the start that morning I felt miserable. I could hardly eat breakfast because every swallow was painful. No matter how carefully I chewed my food, swallowing was a chore; all the food felt like it was jamming up half way down. I had to work each mouthful through to the stomach with a great deal of effort and discomfort. It hurt so badly I actually called the clinic and scheduled an appointment. (When you work in medicine, that's the first sign that something is seriously wrong.)

I was irritable and edgy. No one could get a civil response out of me. This went on till about 9:00 at night. That's when I realized I had failed my attitude test. The testing had come in through the back door of physical pain and caught me unawares. I had to laugh out loud as I recalled my horrible temperament, (and then I had to go and apologize to just about the entire community.)

A Personal Test
Over the next two weeks, things didn't get better. I was busy and happy, but the pain continued. It didn't bother me until I tried to eat or drink something. That same feeling of swallowing thumbtacks and having to work to get them down the last two inches was getting to be a real drag. One night I had a small bite of pizza, and it got stuck for more than five minutes right in the middle of my swallower. Talk about annoying. It was getting to be a real struggle to maintain a good attitude.

I diagnosed myself as having a stricture, which is a narrowing of the muscles in the esophagus. How irritating that I was going to have to go to the clinic, do a bunch of barium swallow x-rays, and then schedule my valuable time to go to the hospital to have some stupid procedure to stretch everything back to where it belonged. If the pain hadn't been getting worse, I don't know if I would have ever gone in.

One's Path can Change in a Heartbeat

The day of my x-rays my whole world turned upside down. When the physician called me at home later that morning, he said that I should come in to his office and talk to him about the x-rays. I knew that was unusual. When I asked if I should have my wife come with me, he quickly said, "Yes, that would be an excellent idea. We need to talk."

In the course of a single afternoon I went from having an annoying pain to waging pitched battle against cancer.

That's when my blood ran cold.

In the course of a single afternoon I went from having an annoying pain to waging pitched battle against cancer. It was clear that I had far worse than a stricture. I was growing a king-sized tumor right there in my esophagus, just above where it meets the stomach.

Who can predict such things? One moment we have one kind of life, and then the next moment that life no longer exists and we are launched into a whole new orbit.

It was a shock to see the x-rays and to talk about the tumor. He was terribly concerned because it was so large there was a great likelihood that it had spread elsewhere, which is very bad. Not only did he tell me that I had acquired a harmful kind of cancer, but if it had spread to the liver or pancreas, he wouldn't even recommend curative treatment; it would be comfort measures only. In one moment I'm trying to accommodate the reality of having cancer and the next I'm thinking, "My God, I've hardly been diagnosed and I'll be going on terminal Hospice care." It was a lot to take in.

There was a series of tests that needed to be done locally, along with the customary journey to the Mayo clinic to get even more tests in order to evaluate how best to proceed. Amidst it all, there were no guarantees. In fact, the one thing that no one wanted to talk about was the fact that although treatments for esophageal cancer have continued to be refined, life expectancy was poor.

Since my cancer had spread to the lymph system, it opened the door to whole new possibilities about where it might be heading, and how long we'd have to try and fight it.

The Cure can be as Hard as the Problem

After everyone had poked and peeked, it was decided that the best way to treat me was chemotherapy and radiation therapy simultaneously, and then to follow with major thoracic surgery to remove the esophagus, a part of the stomach, and a chunk of the nearby lymph system.

When I asked the physician how long this would take he told me that the chemo and radiation would take six weeks, and the surgery would follow about two to four weeks after that. In all, he told me that I would be laid up for six months or longer.

I was stunned. "What about work? I have things to do, a living to make."

He answered curtly, "You have cancer. Forget about it. You have to beat this or you've got nothing." He took on a more compassionate tone. "Once the radiation starts, you won't feel like working. That's the way it is."

Yep, my attitude was getting a real good work out. No doubt about it, all my exhorting and teaching about hope, positive attitudes and overcoming stress were coming home to roost. I either had to live by them, or cast them aside as worthless.

The Choice Was Mine

Let me assure you, there were some mighty tough days. All the things that I normally turned to for security were gone. I had no health, I was in pain (because of the cancer and because of the treatments), I had no work and I brought in no income.

All I could think about were the zillions of projects I hadn't even started, and the many family events I might never get to see. Neither tears nor laughter seemed to make a difference. I had to live this new life day by day, with nothing taken for granted. If I wanted to feel sorry for myself, now was the perfect time to do it.

> *All the things that I normally turned to for security were gone.*

Friends, I can tell you from first hand experience, **where there is life, there is hope.** During all of this, despite the hardships and the lack of guarantees, I picked up my hope and cast my future into God's hands. This wasn't the time to wimp out. It was a time for courage and bold adventure. Surely I would cling to hope. I would anticipate good outcomes even in the face of bad news, and trust that my hope would help me through.

Lessons Learned in Adversity

There are so many lessons I learned through this experience. Here is a simple summary of what I know to be true:

- **Every important decision starts as a declaration.**
  Even when the end is undecided and one has only the ghost of hope to ride upon, that is the time when you have to rise up and make a declaration of what will be. "I will live and not die…"

- **Do your best to have courage.**
  One of my heroes, a 10 year old boy who has been through more surgeries than most encounter in a lifetime, sent me a message through his Mom. "Tell Bob, don't be scared."

  As I was falling asleep under the anesthetic, can you guess what I was thinking?

- **Be a friend and you will have friends.**
  When family, friends, and neighbors rose up and pitched in with help, I was humbled and blessed. I felt that I didn't deserve it, but I certainly was grateful to receive it.

- **It is impossible to pay people back for what they give.**
  This concept was especially hard for me; to recognize that what is freely given never requires payback.

Looking at my life with complete candor, it was easy to see that I had received far more than I had ever put in. Where on earth would I start if I had to pay people back for all that has been given to me? How could I make it right with even one person, let alone the thousands who have contributed to my growth? Life is like a potluck supper. You bring a little something to the table, and you take a little something, but there is a whole lot more for everyone than you could ever make yourself.

➢ **We do not control life or death.**
You can only control yourself – how you will react. It is enough to do that. So do it well, and appreciate all the rest. We always reap whatever it is that we have sown.

Sometimes the best thing that can happen to us is to gather in that old harvest of weeds we've planted and be rid of them, starting over with a fresh season of planting.

➢ **Weather is weather**, whether you like it or not. No one controls the weather, and most can't even predict it.

What is it inside of us that is somehow convinced that every bad occurrence is a consequence to a person's bad behavior? We're just dead sure that any cancer is caused by smoking and only bad people smoke; that every failure in business is caused by mismanagement and only stupid people mismanage; and every broken relationship is caused by mis-communication, and only defective people mis-communicate.

It's preposterous, really. Did you know that in North Dakota when it rains, it rains on the wise and prosperous farmer just as much as it rains on the bad, failing farmer? And when there is a drought, it happens to them all. Weather is weather. What would you think of the person who sticks his head out the window on a rainy day and shouts, "Sorry everybody. If I weren't so evil this wouldn't have happened"? Nor should one take credit for the sunshiny days, "You have me to thank because I was soooo good yesterday."

➤ **In reality, storms simply happen.**

Not everything is triggered by our behavior. I can tell you with a surety that bad choices will lead to bad consequences, but I have been around long enough to know that some really bad choosers appear to be living the high life, while other truly deserving people are simply trying to get through the tempest without perishing. Despite the truth that every person will indeed take in the harvest of what they have sown, weather still happens. It is independent of us. You can't judge a person by the weather.

➤ **It is not helpful to assign blame or to try and figure out what "caused" the cancer.**

What is important is to rise again, and to learn to thrive, even in adverse circumstances. Therefore, remind yourself and others that weather is weather, and quality living is the art of learning to live well no matter what.

Chapter 17: The Three A's for Victory

> **I am not my cancer.**
>
> Cancer does not define me. I am me. I am not even a cancer victim. I am a person who has cancer, but I refuse to be defined by a disease process. Thinking that my disease and I are "one" is bad thinking. The best way I can describe the difference is to say this: I have cancer, the cancer doesn't have me.

> **Attitude is important, and a positive attitude makes a positive difference.**
>
> It's *your* attitude, so it's nobody's business but your own as to what you do with it. If you want a good attitude, you have to make it happen.

I remember so distinctly the day this revelation hit me. I was sitting at the dining room table, reading and reflecting, when I looked over and noticed a heap of dishes in the kitchen sink. I caught myself thinking, "I'm sick. I can't do the dishes." It was as if someone dashed water in my face. "Is this how it's going to be? Is this the new me – the poor sad invalid?" I jumped up and washed every dish I could find, whether it needed it or not. I made a commitment with myself that very hour: I could be sick and miserable, or be sick and positive, and I chose to be positive. Big deal if I was sick. This was my life and I would live it to the full.

You see I wasn't trying to merely survive; I wanted radical, total victory. My hope was completely determined – it would be all or none.

The Three A's

When victory is the order for the day, you need the fuel of the three "A's." If you have these three A's working for you, then you have what it takes to make success. It isn't enough to have just one of them, or to simply know about them.

The three A's are something you have to experience and apply together in order to reap the highest reward. These three A's are:

> *Appetite*
> *Attitude*
> *Altitude*

When the three A's are in alignment, hope runs high and the elements for success are yours in abundance.

Appetite

Appetite is the desire element. To get this you have to answer one simple question: How hungry are you? People that are ferociously hungry will do whatever it takes to eat. Nothing less than food will satisfy. When we want victory, we need that same drive and motivation that only success will satisfy.

The hunger – the appetite – is the burning desire to see our goals accomplished and our problems solved. We simply can't and won't be content with less than total influence, gaining those outcomes that we dearly desire. Appetite is personal. I am full of passion to gain my quest, and I won't settle for anything less.

This isn't gum-chewing hunger or the kind of Thanksgiving Day desire for turkey – this is a downright aching starvation desire to eat. That's the only kind of hunger that will be satisfied because it will not stop until it gets what it wants. Even the overwhelming odds of our enemies (such as ignorance, apathy, hopelessness, and lack of resources) will not deter this appetite. These enemies are only obstacles to overcome not reasons to quit.

In people service this kind of appetite looks like the teacher who insists on learning more and making changes until her whole class succeeds, or the doctor who won't stop with a snap diagnosis, but will push through to find out what's really happening, or the leader who keeps making changes because she has to find a better way, creating a system that works.

Appetite is forceful. If you aren't hungry enough, then get hungry. You'll need it to power you through to the end.

Attitude

The next A for victory is **Attitude**. Our attitude is our positive internal state of knowing that "I" make a difference, and that "WE" can do it. Hope relates to attitude, but attitude does not make hope. They simply work together, like hand and glove. When hope and attitude are in synch – look out world!

I know a lot of folks have a misconception about attitude. They think that a positive attitude is like being Pollyanna, denying reality and playing little glad games to keep one's mind off the horrible realities of life.

I think the better model of positive attitude is "The Little Engine That Could." Any parent that has had to read that story (about 50 – 60 times per child) knows full well that the little engine wasn't designed for the task that lay before it. So many other engines that were better suited for the work felt far too important to go out of their way to help another. The little engine not only took on a job of service, the engine made it work by reciting over and over, "I think I can. I think I can. I think I can."

It was this ability to think positively and to focus single-mindedly on the task at hand that made the little engine succeed. That's the value of attitude. When you stand up and determine with all your soul, "I think I can. I think I can. I think I can," then and only then are you in the right spot for victory.

Good examples of the value of a positive attitude are legion. Any sports star or Wall Street Tycoon will tell the same story; it is essential to have the right attitude. If you allow your attitude to be determined by your circumstances, then you will never get up the gumption and energy to tackle the problems in your life. Those problems will tackle you.

A positive attitude enjoys the abiding belief that what you are trying to do is worth it. Because you know it's worth it, you will try your best to do it the best way you can. When your attitude is right, you know you are a winner and you act according to that knowledge. A great attitude is worth great effort.

Altitude

Finally, the last element for victory is **Altitude**. How high do you want to go? How far do you want to fly? How much do you want – a little or a lot? Will you "settle for" or "set the example?"
Altitude is the element that addresses the completeness of the quest. Victory requires that you be completely sold out. You have set your sights to go higher and farther than anyone else, because you want total victory. Napoleon knew that if he wanted a cannon ball to fly farther, he would have to aim higher. It is the same for us.

Chapter 17: The Three A's for Victory

Altitude will determine your distance.

When Robert Browning said, "… a man's reach should exceed his grasp…" he was talking about altitude.

Is your altitude set high enough to make a difference? You can have an appetite and the right attitude, but if you only aim at the height you can easily make, you will fall short of all you might have accomplished.

At first altitude is in proportion to the other two. As we grow and struggle and yearn, even though we may not appear to win, we discover that our altitude can be set progressively higher. Even our failures grant us the experience we need to do more and climb higher.

Our altitude may start with only influencing one person, (like our self), and then grow to a couple of people, to a family, a neighborhood, a town, a state, a nation, a world.

Is your altitude high enough to make a difference?

Once again, we have come full circle to the beginning of our hope, which is the OUTCOME WE ENVISION.

IT MAY BE ERADICATING A DISEASE,
  TEACHING TO READ,
    FEEDING THE POOR,
      CLEANING UP A DISASTER,
        MINISTERING TO A BODY,
          OR REDISCOVERING THE ROOTS OF ALL THAT IS PRECIOUS IN THE HUMAN SOUL.

The strength of your purpose is the strength of your hope.

A life of hope is often lived in the face of daunting odds. There are no guarantees, but we don't need them in order to have hope. What we need is purpose, vision, and desire.

Life isn't about self-improvement - **it's about living well.**

The three A's are essential elements for victory. Without hope we will certainly miss the satisfaction of making a difference. With hope we may miss our goals, but we will never miss the worth hope brings to living.

Chapter XVIII

Hope From the Heart

In which we say goodbye with the certain knowledge that hope is worth the effort. Where there's life, there's hope.

You have a lot in common with Alexander the Great and George Washington – you don't have a clue what tomorrow will bring.

Even so, your tomorrow may well contain the victory you eagerly seek. That is the very ground of hope. Your hope is so important, because hope is the wellspring of all the good things of life.

Tomorrow is not a logical extension of today; it is a fresh commodity that hasn't been touched, a chapter that hasn't been written. Time and chance always come in play, and no one knows whether this thing or that will succeed. You may well be only a day away from significant achievement.

Often it's what we don't see and don't know that ushers in our greatest blessings, (and sometimes our greatest and scariest challenges). We may fear the unknown, but hope leads us to anticipate good rather than ill. When we are so frightened we give up in abject surrender, we aren't using our hope. Instead, we are basing our actions upon our restricted assessment – which is limited knowledge. When it comes to tomorrow, we really don't know anything at all.

Friends, we can't ever know it all.

Mom Was Right

Where there is life there is hope. As long as we can draw breath, we have reasons to hope. There is always a risk to life, but a life of despair is far worse than the risk of missing the target. Think of all the hopeful losers you can, and ask yourself this: Did their hope mock them when they lost, or did it help them rise again to face the new day?

Well it was that Winston Churchill's famous speech to a graduating class consisted of only these words:

> "Never, never, never, never, never, give in."

Your life is like a sailing vessel, and you can assemble the five critical parts that equip you to sail through the circumstances of life. With the various elements of hope in place, you can use the very things that life throws at you, and you can chart a course that is unique to you. No matter how rough it may be, hope will keep you afloat.

Hope is an essential component of quality living. Hope itself becomes the fertile ground out of which our beliefs can be transformed. Since we make choices in accordance with what we believe, we need to get our beliefs to coincide with what we want – to support our purpose in life.

To sail from "here to there" we have to assert our will. This is not pretending, it is DECIDING. Such an optimistic outlook doesn't deny reality; it simply denies the finality of it.

Therefore, a hope-full life starts with an act of the will, with your free decision to be a woman or man of hope. You say to yourself,

> *"I **will** hope that good will come to me, that I am capable of doing good and being good, and free to make the changes I need in order to reach the destination I deeply desire."*

As you endure in this hope, circumstances may well rise against you, testing you and your resolve. The ocean is full of wind and wave. You will undoubtedly have failures but you will also enjoy success. It is not for nothing that King Solomon said, "The end of a matter is better than its beginning." You simply have to live through the learning curve to install the truth.

In truth, you will discover more than enough hope for yourself. **You will have hope to share.** There are so many people in this world that need **YOU** to be full of hope. There are so many who need **YOU** to fulfill your purpose and pursue your vision.

St. Francis of Assisi, over 800 years ago, made this profound observation:

**"Start by doing what is necessary,
    then what is possible,
        and suddenly you're doing the impossible."**

It's just as true today as when he first spoke it. Dare to hope, because you are worth it. There is a reason you are here, and I can hardly . wait to see it revealed.

After all, life isn't about self-improvement - it's about living well.

So live a little, and hope a lot

Additional Reading

Biehl, Bobb. *Stop Setting Goals If You Would Rather Solve Problems.* Nashville: Moorings, 1995.

Harrell, Keith. *Attitude is Everything.* New York: HarperCollins, 2000.

Jones, Laurie Beth. *The Path: Creating Your Mission Statement for Work and Life.* New York: Hyperion, 1996.

Kolbe, Kathy. *The Conative Connection: Uncovering the Link Between Who You Are and How You Perform.* Reading: Addison-Wesley, 1990.

Perry, J. Mitchell, with Griggs, Richard E. *The Road to Optimism.* San Ramon, CA: Manfit Press, 1997.

Seligman, Martin E. P. Ph.D. *Learned Optimism: How to Change Your Mind and Your Life.* New York: Pocket Books, 1998.

Silvoso, Ed. *Anointed for Business.* Ventura: Regal Books, 2002.

Index

A
Acceptable level of mediocrity, 92
Achievement, 198
Action process, 145
Alcoholics Anonymous, 100
Alexander the Great, 68, 215
Altitude, 212
Americans with Disabilities Act, 87
"*Anticipation*", 130
Anticipation, 128
Appetite, 210
Association, 196
Attitude, 211
Autonomy, 197

B
"Best Practice", 145
Boom:
   described, 22
   function of, 23
Browning, Robert, 19, 213
Buoyancy, 20
Bryan, William Jennings, 132

C
Can vs. can't, 145
Change:
   compared to serpent, 40
   compared to rudder, 29
   everyone can, 54
   perception of, 42
   resisted, 41
Change making, 29
Choice making, 28
Churchill, Sir Winston, 216
Columbus, Christopher, 134
Compound interest, 95
Conative Connection, The, 160
Continental Army, 176
Continuous learning, 138
Control:
   compared to sailing, 26
   described, 53
   examples of, 56, 184

D
Darius, King, 69
Declaration of Independence, 94, 176
Denial, 189
Depression, 15
Desire:
   compared to mast, 27
   description, 169
   function of, 167-169
Destiny, 132
Detailed vision statement, 124
Disney, Walt, 114
Doldrums:
   compared to circumstances, 31
   lack of energy, 26
Drucker, Peter F., 138

E
Endurance, 182
Enthusiasm, 172
Entropy, 91
Esophageal cancer, 203
Exclusive language, 187
Exercise, 196
Expectations, 129

F
Feedback, 138-140
Final solution, 80
Flexibility:
   contrasted to boom, 23
   described, 23
Floatation:
   contrasted to hope, 27
   function of, 23, 27
Free will, 42, 54
Free:
   free from, 55
   frce to, 56
Fun, 199

G
Gandhi, 155
Gaugamela, 69
Girl Scouts, 196
God, 101, 200

H
Higher Power, 100
Hitler, 43
HOBY, 171
Hope:
   anticipates, 128

Hope (continued)
  caring, 169
  defined, 20
  fed by progress, 194
  feedback, 188
  first lesson of, 46
  greater than circumstances, 75
  holistic, 74
  is a choice, 178
  is a condition, 76
  is catchy, 144
  is real, 176
  measuring of, 136
  mission, 111
  motivated by will, 163
  purpose, 115
  quality of life, 170
  related to attitude, 211
  second lesson of, 53
  share it, 121
  third lesson of, 65
  vision, 118
"*Hope Floats*", 20
Hugh O'Brian Youth Leadership, 171

I
Identity:
  contrasted to keel, 28
  definite advantage, 110
  new mother, 107
  not your circumstances, 75
  western ideas of, 108
Inclusive language, 187
Inertia Exercise, 86

J
Jefferson City, 117
Jenkins' Law, 163
Jibing, 25
Judgment, 159

K
Keel:
  contrasted to identity, 28
  function of, 24
King George, 178
Kolbe, Kathy, 160

L
Laughter:
  antidote to stress, 57
  statistics, 59
Law of motion, 85
Learned helplessness, 154
"*Learned Optimism*", 182
Learning curve, 55, 73, 107
Life:
  belongs to you, 32
  choose it, 27
  compared to sailboat, 30
"*Little Engine That Could*", 211
Locus of control:
  external, 66
  internal, 66
Luff/luffing, 156

M
Mast:
  compared to desire, 28
  function of, 23
Mayo Clinic, 204
Measuring/measurement, 135-137
Mediocrity, 92
Menninger Clinic, 41
Minneapolis, 135
Minnesota, 21, 135
Mission statement, 113
Missouri, 117
Mother Teresa, 155
Motivation, 163
Mussolini, 43

N
Native Americans, 119
Nazi, 43
Newton, Sir Isaac, 85
North Dakota, 38, 119, 208

O
Oppression, 43
Optimism, related to hope, 182, 189
Outcomes, 136, 213

P
Patience, 99
Pearl Harbor, 68
Permanence, 183

Perry, Dr. J. Mitchell, 187, 189
Perseverance, 182
Persistence, 182
Personal mission statement, 113
Personal vision statement, 123
Pervasiveness, 183
Pessimism, 182-184
Physical activity, 196
Plan/plans, 150
Polaris, 136
Purpose:
  described, 112, 115
  for others, 126
  identity and, 106
  creates desire, 170

Q
Quality life/living:
  described, 29
  hope essential, 171
  need for, 170
Queen Isabella, 134

R
Rest, 195
Results, 140
"*The Road to Optimism*", 187
Rudder, function of, 24
Rugby, 38, 117
Rule of 72, 95

S
Sailing:
  compared to living, 27
  five required elements, 22
  into the wind, 24
Sails:
  compared to will, 27, 163
  function of, 23
Seligman, Dr. Martin, 14, 182
St. Francis, 217
Stress:
  cost of, 51
  defined, 50

T
Tacking, 24, 104
Task shift, 140
Tito, 43
True North, 135
Twelve step program, 100

U
Unconditional love, 110
Unknown, 65

V
Valley Forge, 176-178
Values:
  of commitment, 13
  of excellence, 13
  of service, 13
Vision Statements:
  compared to rudder, 131
  described, 122
  detailed, 123
  example, 118, 124
  get one, 131
  read out loud, 190
Vision:
  described, 128
  direction and, 127
  for others, 121, 126
  hope and, 127
  love and, 126
Volition, 160

W
War of Independence, 94
Washington, George, 176, 215
Will:
  described, 153, 157, 159
  example of, 161
  makes action, 157, 161
  motivates hope, 163
  staying power of, 160
Writing:
  mission statements, 114
  vision statements, 121

XYZ
Y2K, 37
Yugoslavia, 43

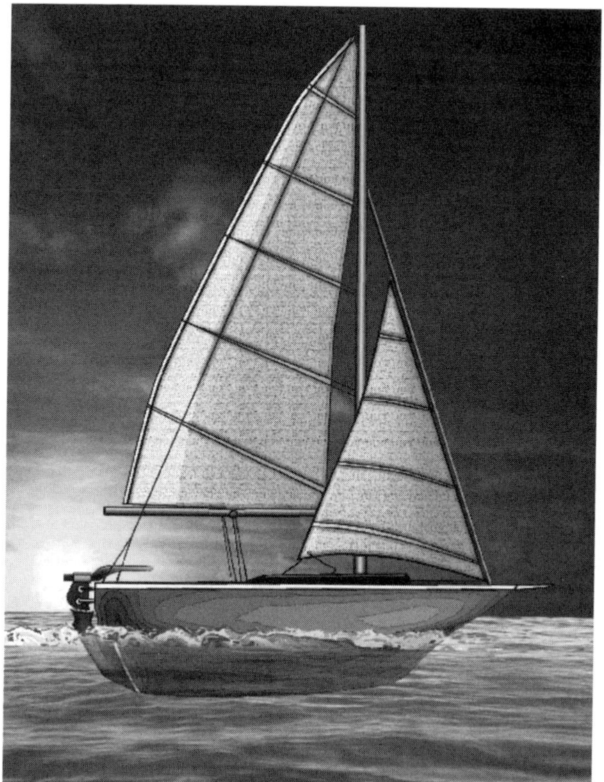

About the Author

Robert "Bob" Jenkins, President of Jenkins & Associates, knows the practical value of "catching your vision" and most importantly, "living your vision." Serving as a consultant and advocate for organizational effectiveness, Bob helps individuals and organizations discover and implement their purpose through investment in people.

- ➢ Establishing purpose and outcomes
- ➢ Team confidence and performance
- ➢ Creating intelligent "feedback"
- ➢ Empowering people with purpose to do their real work with real achievement

With over 25 years as a Healthcare Executive, Bob has worked in rural Hospitals and Long Term Care settings. He is a Certified Nursing Home Administrator (ACHCA), Coordinator of the State Administrator-in-Training program, and recipient of the North Dakota Administrator of the Year 2000, and the Distinguished Service Award 2002.

Often entertaining, always informative, Bob breaks complex and dynamic issues into insightful principles that you can use at work and in life – principles of purpose-driven service and strategy that help you "Build Your Advantage." ™

> At heart, he is a singer and actor - and dancer only when mandatory. He is also a creative writer. In his spare time he guest stars as the father of five and husband of one.